GIANT BOOK OF KNOCK-KNOCK JOKES

By
Ronny M. Cole
Joseph Rosenbloom

Illustrations By
Joyce Behr · Rich Garramone
Sandy Hoffman

Sterling Publishing Company, Inc.
New York

10 9 8 7 6 5 4 3 2

Published by Sterling Publishing Company, Inc.
387 Park Avenue South, New York, N.Y. 10016

Material in this collection was adapted from
Doctor Knock-Knock's & Nutty Knock Knocks!
© Joseph Rosenbloom
Zany Knock Knocks © Ronny M. Cole

Distributed in Canada by Sterling Publishing
c/o Canadian Manda Group, One Atlantic Avenue, Suite 105
Toronto, Ontario, Canada M6K 3E7

Distributed in Great Britain and Europe by Chris Lloyd
463 Ashley Road, Parkstone, Poole, Dorset, BH14 0AX,
United Kingdom

Distributed in Australia by Capricorn Link (Australia) Pty Ltd
P.O. Box 6651, Baulkham, Business Centre, NSW 2153, Australia

Sterling ISBN 0-8069-2075-0

CONTENTS

Knock-Knock!

Knock–knock.
    Who's there?
Aardvark.
    Aardvark who?
Aardvark-um cleaner broke.
Can I borrow yours?

Knock–knock.
    Who's there?
Aaron.
    Aaron who?
Why Aaron you
opening the door?

Knock–knock.
    Who's there?
Abbey.
    Abbey who?
Abbey Birthday!

Knock–knock.
　Who's there?
Abe.
　Abe who?
Abe out face!

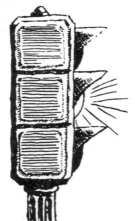

Knock–knock.
　Who's there?
Abe Lincoln.
　Abe Lincoln who?
Abe Lincoln (a blinkin')
yellow light means
slow down!

Knock–knock.
　Who's there?
Abyssinia.
　Abyssinia who?
Abyssinia at the mall!

Knock–knock.
　Who's there?
Abercrombie.
　Abercrombie who?
Abercrombie (have a
crumby) time at the
party!

Knock–knock.
　Who's there?
Acey Ducey.
　Acey Ducey who?
Acey your point, Ducey
mine?

Knock–knock.
　Who's there?
Achilles.
　Achilles who?
Achilles mosquitoes
with a swatter! (*Slap!*)

Knock–knock.
Who's there?
Ada.
Ada who?
You're Ada your mind.

Knock–knock.
Who's there?
Adam.
Adam who?
Adam my way—
I"m coming in!

Knock–knock.
Who's there?
Addison.
Addison who?
Addison no way to treat
an old friend.

Knock–knock.
Who's there?
Afghan.
Afghan who?
Afghan away and never
see you again.

Knock–knock.
Who's there?
Agate.
Agate who?
Agate you covered!

Knock–knock.
Who's there?
Afghanistan.
Afghanistan who?
Afghanistan out here
all night if you don't
open the door.

Knock–knock.
Who's there?
Aiken.
Aiken who?
Oh, my Aiken back!

Knock–knock.
Who's there?
A la mode.
A la mode who?
Remember the
A la mode (Alamo)!

Knock–knock.
Who's there?
Al and Edith.
Al and Edith who?
"Al and Edith love . . ."

Knock–knock.
Who's there?
Albee.
Albee who?
Albee a monkey's
uncle!

Knock–knock.
Who's there?
Alcott.
Alcott who?
Alcott the cake.
You pour the tea.

Knock–knock.
Who's there?
Alda.
Alda who?
Alda time you knew
who it was!

Knock–knock.
Who's there?
Alda and Alda.
Alda and Alda who?
I'm getting Alda and Alda
standing out here in the
cold.

Knock–knock.
Who's there?
Aldo.
Aldo who?
Aldo anything for you.

Knock–knock.
Who's there?
Aldus.
Aldous who?
Aldous fuss over little ol' me?

Knock–knock.
Who's there?
Aldus.
Aldous who?
Aldous knocking is giving me a headache.

Knock–knock.
Who's there?
Aldus.
Aldus who?
Aldus talk and no action!

Knock–knock.
Who's there?
Alec.
Alec who?
Alec-tricity. Isn't that a shock?

Knock–knock.
Who's there?
Alex.
Alex who?
Alex-plain later. Open the door.

Knock–knock.
Who's there?
Alex.
Alex who?
Alex the questions around here.

Knock–knock.
Who's there?
Alfalfa.
Alfalfa who?
Alfalfa (I'll fall for) you,
if you blow in my ear.

Knock–knock.
Who's there?
Alfie.
Alfie who?
Alfie-give your rudeness—I
know you're just being
yourself.

Knock–knock.
Who's there?
Ali.
Ali who?
Ali time you
knew it was me.

Knock–knock.
Who's there?
Alistair.
Alistar who?
You uncover the pot,
Alistair the soup!

Knock–knock.
Who's there?
Alfie.
Alfie who?
Alfie you in my dreams.

Knock–knock.
Who's there?
Alice.
Alice who?
Alice fair in love
and war!

Knock–knock.
　Who's there?
Alma.
　Alma who?
The dog ate Alma
homework!

Knock–knock.
　Who's there?
Alma Gibbons.
　Alma Gibbons who?
Alma Gibbons you 24 hours
to get out of town.

Knock–knock.
　Who's there?
Aloha.
　Aloha who?
Aloha, there!

Knock–knock.
　Who's there?
Althea.
　Althea who?
Althea in jail!

Knock–knock.
　Who's there?
Altoona.
　Altoona who?
Altoona piano–you play it!

Knock–knock.
　Who's there?
Alva and Alma.
　Alva and Alma who?
Alva day long I spend
Alma time outside your door.

Knock–knock.
　Who's there?
Alyce.
　Alyce who?
Alyce thought you
were nuts.

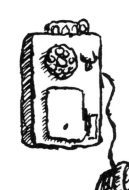

Knock–knock.
　Who's there?
Amahl.
　Amahl who?
Amahl tied up,
call me later!

A

Knock–knock.
Who's there?
Amana.
Amana who?
Amana-eating tiger!

Knock–knock.
Who's there?
Amanda Lynn.
Amanda Lynn who?
Amanda Lynn player.

Knock–knock.
Who's there?
Amarillo.
Amarillo who?
Amarillo nice guy.

Knock–knock.
 Who's there?
Amaryllis.
 Amaryllis who?
Amaryllis-state agent.
Want to buy a house?

Knock–knock.
 Who's there?
Toboggan.
 Toboggan who?
Yes, but I don't like toboggan.

Knock–knock.
 Who's there?
Arlo.
 Arlo who?
Arlo prices can't be beat.

Knock–knock.
    Who's there?
Amateur.
        Amateur who?
Amateur service.

Knock–knock.
    Who's there?
Amerigo.
        Amerigo who?
Amerigo-round.

    Knock–knock.
        Who's there?
    Vespucci.
            Vespucci who?
    How much is Vespucci (that poochie) in the window?

Knock–knock.
Who's there?
Amen.
Amen who?
Amen hot water
again.

Knock–knock.
Who's there?
Amish.
Amish who?
Amish you sho mush!

Knock–knock.
Who's there?
Amnesia.
Amnesia who?
Oh, I see you have it, too!

Knock–knock.
Who's there?
Amoeba.
Amoeba who?
"Amoeba wrong,
but I think you're
wonderful . . ."

Knock–knock.
Who's there?
Anastasia.
Anastasia who?
Anastasia out here
in the rain.

Knock–knock.
Who's there?
Anatol.
Anatol who?
Anatol you what
I thought of you.

Knock–knock.
Who's there?
Andalusia.
Andalusia who?
I'd like to take you
someplace Andalusia.

Knock–knock.
Who's there?
Andante.
Andante who?
I'm going to visit my
uncle Andante too.

Knock–knock.
Who's there?
Andy Green.
Andy Greeen who?
"Andy Green grass grows
all around, all around . . ."

Knock–knock.
 Who's there?
Anita.
 Anita who?
Anita rest!

Knock–knock.
 Who's there?
Angela.
 Angela who?
Angela Mercy.

Knock–knock.
 Who's there?
Anna Maria Alberghetti.
 Anna Maria Alberghetti who?
"Anna Maria Alberghetti in a taxi, honey . . . "

Knock–knock.
 Who's there?
Anna Mary.
 Anna Mary who?
"Anna Mary old soul was he . . ."

Knock–knock.
 Who's there?
Annapolis.
 Annapolis who?
Annapolis day keeps the doctor away.

Knock–knock.
 Who's there?
Annie.
 Annie who?
Annie-body alive in there?

Knock–knock.
　Who's there?
Antilles.
　Antilles who?
Antilles open the door,
I'm gonna sit here on
your doorstep!

Dracula: **Knock–knock.**
　Victim: Who's there?
Dracula: A-One.
　Victim: A-One who?
Dracular: A-One to drink
　　　　your blood.

Knock–knock.
　Who's there?
Apollo.
　Apollo who?
Any Apollo yours
is Apollo mine.

Knock–knock.
　Who's there?
Archer.
　Archer who?
Archer glad to see
me?

Knock–knock.
　Who's there?
Arcudi.
　Arcudi who?
Arcudi little dog
can do one trick.

Knock–knock.
Who's there?
Ariel.
Ariel who?
You're Ariel pain
in the neck!

Knock–knock.
Who's there?
Armada.
Armada who?
Armada told us there'd
be days like this.

Knock–knock.
Who's there?
Armand.
Armand who?
Armand the outside
looking inside.

Knock–knock.
Who's there?
Armstrong.
Armstrong who?
Armstrong as an ox—
and you have the brain
of one.

Knock–knock.
Who's there?
Arne.
Arne who?
Arne you going
to ask me in?

Knock–knock.
Who's there?
Arno.
Arno who?
Arno kids to play
with, so I'm bored.

Knock–knock.
 Who's there?
Arsenio Hall.
 Arsenio Hall who?
Arsenio Hall (I've seen
you all) over town!

Knock–knock.
 Who's there?
Artichoke.
 Artichoke who?
Artichoke on a chicken bone.

Knock–knock.
 Who's there?
Artie Fish.
 Artie Fish who?
Artie Fish-el intelligence!

Knock–knock.
Who's there?
Aruba.
Aruba who?
Aruba (are you the)
one in charge?

Knock–knock.
Who's there?
Asbestos.
Asbestos who?
I'm doing Asbestos I can!

Knock–knock.
Who's there?
Aruba.
Aruba who?
Aruba your back,
you rub'a mine.

Knock–knock.
Who's there?
Ashur.
Ashur who?
Ashur wish you'd
open this door.

Knock–knock.
Who's there?
Ashley.
Ashley who?
Ashley, I'm not sure . . .

Knock–knock.
    Who's there?
Asta.
    Asta who?
Asta La Veesta, baby!

Knock–knock.
    Who's there?
Asthma.
    Asthma who?
Asthma no questions.
      Knock–knock.
        Who's there?
Attila.
      Attila who?
Attila no lies.

Knock–knock.
    Who's there?
Astoria.
    Astoria who?
I've got Astoria wouldn't believe!
    Knock–knock.
        Who's there?
Boris.
        Boris who?
Go ahead, Boris with another story!

Knock–knock.
    Who's there?
Attila.
    Attila who?
Attila we meet again!

Knock–knock.
    Who's there?
Atwood.
    Atwood who?
Atwood be nice if
you asked me in.

Knock–knock.
    Who's there?
Aubrey.
    Aubrey who?
Aubrey Quiet!

Knock–knock.
Who's there?
Auerbach.
Auerbach who?
Please scratch
Auerbach.

Knock–knock.
Who's there?
Aunt Lou.
Aunt Lou who?
Aunt Lou do you
think you are?

Knock–knock.
Who's there?
Autumn.
Autumn who?
You Autumn mind
your own business!

Knock–knock.
Who's there?
Ava.
Ava who?
Ava seen you
someplace before?

Knock–knock.
Who's there?
Avenue.
Avenue who?
Avenue been missing me?

Knock–knock.
Who's there?
Avis.
Avis who?
Avis just at the zoo
and thought about you.

Knock–knock.
Who's there?
Avenue.
Avenue who?
Avenue heard the good news

Knock–knock.
    Who's there?
Avocado.
    Avocado who?
Avocado cold. Thad's
why I dalk dis way.

Knock–knock.
    Who's there?
Avon.
    Avon who?
Avon to be alone.

Knock-Knock!

B

Knock–knock.
Who's there?
Babylon.
Babylon who?
Babylon–I'm not listening anyway!

Knock–knock.
Who's there?
Babbit.
Babbit who?
Babbit and Costello!

Knock–knock.
Who's there?
Bach.
Bach who?
Bach to the future!

Knock–knock.
Who's there?
Bacilli.
Bacilli who?
Don't bacilli!

Knock–knock.
Who's there?
Baldoni.
Baldoni who?
Baldoni a little on the top.

Knock–knock.
Who's there?
Banana.
Banana who?
Banana messages
for me?

Knock–knock.
Who's there?
Barbara.
Barbara who?
"Barbara black sheep,
have you any wool . . ."

Knock–knock.
Who's there?
Barbara.
Barbara who?
The Barbara Seville.

Knock–knock.
Who's there?
Barbie.
Barbie who?
Barbie Q. Chicken.

Knock–knock.
Who's there?
B.C.
B.C. who?
B.C'ing you!

Knock–knock.
Who's there?
Bea.
Bea who?
Bea Faroni!

Knock–knock.
Who's there?
Beecher.
Beecher who?
Beecher at any game
you pick.

Knock–knock.
    Who's there?
Beehive.
    Beehive who?
Beehive yourself!

Knock–knock.
    Who's there?
Bella.
    Bella who?
Bella bottom trousers.

Knock–knock.
    Who's there?
Belladonna.
    Belladonna who?
Belladonna work, so I
had to knock.

Knock–knock.
    Who's there?
Ben and Anna.
    Ben and Anna who?
Ben and Anna split
so ice creamed.

Knock–knock.
    Who's there?
Belle Lee.
    Belle Lee who?
Belle Lee Dancer.

Knock–knock.
    Who's there?
Benny.
    Benny who?
Benny long time
no see.

Knock–knock.
Who's there?
Beryl.
Beryl who?
Beryl of monkeys.

Knock–knock.
Who's there?
Betty.
Betty who?
Betty B. Careful!

Knock–knock.
Who's there?
Blake.
Blake who?
Blake a leg!

Knock–knock.
Who's there?
Bertha.
Bertha who?
Bertha-day greetings.

Knock–knock.
Who's there?
Beth.
Beth who?
Beth wisheth, thweetie.

Knock–knock.
Who's there?
Betty.
Betty who?
Betty-Bye!

Knock–knock.
Who's there?
Blubber.
Blubber who?
"Blubber, come back to me . . ."

Knock–knock.
　　Who's there?
Bob Dwyer.
　　Bob Dwyer who?
Bob Dwyer out here.
Caught my pants on it.
　　Knock–knock.
　　　Who's there?
Apache.
　　　Apache who?
Apache them for
you.

Knock–knock.
　　Who's there?
Boise.
　　Boise who?
Boise strange!
　　Knock–knock.
　　　Who's there?
Idaho.
　　　Idaho who?
Idaho. I've seen
stranger.

Knock–knock.
   Who's there?
Boll weevil.
   Boll weevil who?
After the boll weevil
all go home.

Knock–knock.
   Who's there?
Brigham.
   Brigham who?
Brigham a present!

Knock–knock.
   Who's there?
Brighton.
   Brighton who?
Up Brighton early
just to see you.

Knock–knock.
   Who's there?
Brinckerhoff.
   Brinckerhoff who?
You Brinckerhoff the soda—
I'll bring the other half.

Knock–knock.
　Who's there?
Bruno.
　Bruno who?
Bruno who it is!

Knock–knock.
　Who's there?
Britches.
　Britches who?
"London Britches
falling down . . ."

Knock–knock.
　Who's there?
Buck.
　Buck who?
"Buck, buck!" I'm a chicken.

Knock–knock.
　Who's there?
Adelaide.
　Adelaide who?
Adelaide an egg.

Knock-knock.
　Who's there?
Eggs.
　Eggs who?
Eggs-tremely cold out here
in the chicken house.

Knock–knock.
    Who's there?
Buck and Ham.
    Buck and Ham who?
Buck and Ham Palace!

Knock–knock.
    Who's there?
Budapest.
    Budapest who?
You're nothing
Budapest.

Knock–knock.
    Who's there?
Butcher.
    Butcher who?
"Butcher head on my
shoulder . . ."

Knock-Knock!

Knock–knock.
  Who's there?
Caesar.
  Caesar who?
"Caesar jolly good
fellow . . ."

Knock–knock.
  Who's there?
Cain and Abel.
    Cain and Abel who?
Cain talk now—
Abel tomorrow.

Knock–knock.
  Who's there?
Cain.
  Cain who?
Cain you hear me?
Knock-Knock!

Knock–knock.
  Who's there?
Calder.
    Calder who?
Calder police–
I've been robbed!

Knock–knock.
  Who's there?
Camellia.
    Camellia who?
Camellia little closer.

Knock–knock.
Who's there?
Candace.
Candace who?
Candace snake do
push-ups?

38

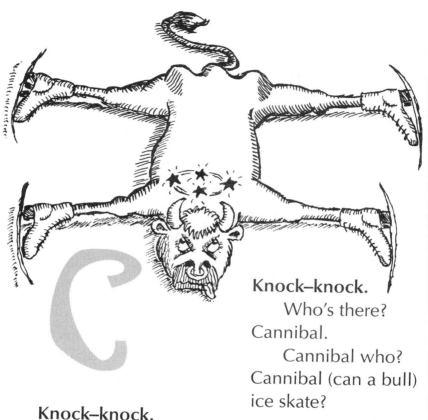

C

Knock–knock.
　Who's there?
Candice.
　　Candice who?
Candice be love?

Knock–knock.
　Who's there?
Cantaloupe.
　　Cantaloupe who?
Cantaloupe today,
maybe tomorrow . . .

Knock–knock.
　Who's there?
Cannibal.
　　Cannibal who?
Cannibal (can a bull)
ice skate?

Knock–knock.
　Who's there?
Cannibal.
　　Cannibal who?
Cannibal-eve you're
for real!

Knock–knock.
　Who's there?
Cantillo.
　　Cantillo who?
Cantillo my name,
but my face will be familiar.

Knock–knock.
Who's there?
Canoe.
Canoe who?
Canoe please
get off my foot?

Knock–knock.
Who's there?
Carew.
Carew who?
The Carew of the
Love Boat.

Knock–knock.
Who's there?
Carina.
Carina who?
Carina ditch. Can I
use your phone?

Knock–knock.
Who's there?
Caribbean.
Caribbean who?
You don't Caribbean
that I'm standing out
here in a snowstorm.

Knock–knock.
Who's there?
Carmen.
Carmen who?
"Carmen to my parlor,"
said the spider to the fly!

Knock–knock.
Who's there?
Carmen or Cohen.
Carmen or Cohen who?
You don't know whether
you're Carmen or Cohen.

Knock–knock.
Who's there?
Carrie.
Carrie who?
Carrie R. pigeon.

Knock–knock.
Who's there?
Carrie.
Carrie who?
Carrie me inside–
I'm tired.

Knock–knock.
Who's there?
Carmencita.
Carmencita who?
Carmencita down and take
a load off your feet.

Knock–knock.
Who's there?
Casanova.
Casanova who?
Casanova (isn't over)
until the fat lady sings.

Knock–knock.
Who's there?
Cashew.
Cashew who?
Cashew see I'm busy?

Knock–knock.
Who's there?
Cashew.
Cashew who?
Cashew see it's me?

Knock–knock.
Who's there?
Cass.
Cass who?
Cass Toff, we're leaving!

Knock–knock.
Who's there?
Cassie.
Cassie who?
Cassie Nova!
How can you
resist me?

C

Knock–knock.
Who's there?
Cassie.
Cassie who?
Cassie O. Watch!

Knock–knock.
Who's there?
Cassie.
Cassie who?
Cassie you know–
I've got to run!

Knock–knock.
Who's there?
Cassius.
Cassius who?
Cassius if you can!

Knock–knock.
Who's there?
Cattle Drive.
Cattle Drive who?
This Cattle (cat will)
Drive you crazy!

Knock–knock.
Who's there?
Cecilius.
Cecilius who?
Cecilius Knock–Knock
joke I ever heard.

Knock–knock.
Who's there?
Celeste.
Celeste who?
Celeste time I saw a face
like yours, I threw it a fish.

Knock–knock.
Who's there?
Celeste.
Celeste who?
Celeste you know
the better!

Knock–knock.
Who's there?
Celia.
Celia who?
Celia later, alligator!

Knock–knock.
Who's there?
Charlotta.
Charlotta who?
Charlotta fuss about
nothing.

Knock–knock.
Who's there?
Cher.
Cher who?
Cher-lock Holmes.

Knock–knock.
　Who's there?
Cheese.
　Cheese who?
Cheese a cute girl.

Knock–knock.
　Who's there?
Cher.
　Cher who?
Cher would be nice
if you opened the door!

Knock–knock.
　Who's there?
Cherry.
　Cherry who?
Cherry Lewis!

Knock–knock.
　Who's there?
Chicken.
　Chicken who?
Just Chicken out the
doorbell!

C

Knock–knock.
Who's there?
Chesapeake.
Chesapeake who?
Chesapeake to me and
I'll tell you everything.

Knock–knock.
Who's there?
Chess game.
Chess game who?
Chess game to say
goodbye.

Knock–knock.
Who's there?
Chester.
Chester who?
"Chester song at
twilight . . ."

Knock–knock.
Who's there?
Chester.
Chester who?
Chester little kid!

Knock–knock.
Who's there?
Chesterfield.
Chesterfield who?
Chesterfield my leg, so
I slapped him.

Knock–knock.
Who's there?
Chihuahua (pronounced Chi-*wah*-wah).
Chihuahua who?
Chihuahua buy a magazine subscription?

Knock–knock.
Who's there?
Cinnamon.
Cinnamon who?
Cinnamon-ster–
shut the door!

Knock–knock.
Who's there?
Colin.
Colin who?
Colin the doctor!
You make me sick.

Knock-knock.
Who's there?
Colleen.
Colleen who?
Colleen all cars!

Knock–knock.
    Who's there?
Cologne.
        Cologne who?
Cologne Ranger!

Knock–knock.
    Who's there?
Collie.
        Collie who?
Collie a taxi. I'm
leaving.

Knock–knock.
    Who's there?
Comma.
        Comma who?
"Comma up and
see me sometime."

Knock–knock.
    Who's there?
Concha.
        Concha who?
Concha hear me knocking?

Knock–knock.
Who's there?
Costanza.
Costanza who?
Costanza out here in the rain. Open up!

Knock–knock.
Who's there?
Culligan.
Culligan who?
I'll Culligan when you have something intelligent to say.

Knock–knock.
Who's there?
Cotton.
Cotton who?
Cotton off to a bad start!

Knock–knock.
Who's there?
Combat.
Combat who?
Combat tomorrow!

Knock–knock.
Who's there?
Crassus.
Crassus who?
Crassus always greener on the other side!

Knock–knock.
Who's there?
Cosmo.
Cosmo who?
You Cosmo trouble than anybody I know.

Knock–knock.
Who's there?
Culver.
Culver who?
Culver me up, I'm freezing.

Knock–knock.
　Who's there?
Cy.
　Cy who?
Cy knew it was you, I wouldn't have bothered knocking.

Knock–knock.
　Who's there?
Czar.
　Czar who?
Czar-y about that!
Knock–knock.
　Who's there?
Apollo.
　Apollo who?
Apollo G. Accepted!

Knock-knock.
　Who's there?
Czar.
　Czar who?
Czar a doctor in the house?

Knock-Knock!

D

Knock–knock.
    Who's there?
Dakar.
    Dakar who?
Dakar has a flat tire!

Knock–knock.
    Who's there?
Dakota.
    Dakota who?
Dakota many colors.

Knock–knock.
    Who's there?
Damascus.
    Damascus who?
Damascus slipping off da face.

Knock–knock.
  Who's there?
Danielle.
  Danielle who?
Danielle at me, I heard
you the first time.

Knock–knock.
  Who's there?
Darby.
  Darby who?
Darby a lot of reasons
why I knocked.

  Knock–knock.
    Who's there?
  Darren.
    Darren who?
  Darren you to
  open the door!

Knock–knock.
  Who's there?
Dandelion.
  Dandelion who?
Dandelion around out here,
but open the door anyway.

Knock–knock.
  Who's there?
Dancer.
  Dancer who?
"Dancer, my friend, is
blowing in the wind . . ."

Knock–knock.
   Who's there?
Darth Vader.
   Darth Vader who?
Darth Vader cookie crumbles.

Knock–knock.
　　Who's there?
Darwin.
　　Darwin who?
I'll be Darwin
(there when)
you open the door.

Knock–knock.
　　Who's there?
Daryl.
　　Daryl who?
"Daryl never ever
be another you . . ."

Knock–knock.
　　Who's there?
Data.
　　Data who?
Data new hairdo or
did you just walk
through a car wash?

Knock–knock.
　　Who's there?
Datsun.
　　Datsun who?
Datsun old joke.

54

Knock–knock.
Who's there?
Daughter.
Daughter who?
Daughter-door salesman!

Knock–knock.
Who's there?
Dawn.
Dawn who?
Dawn do anything
I wouldn't do.

Knock–knock.
Who's there?
Deanna.
Deanna who?
"Till Deanna time . . ."

Knock–knock.
Who's there?
Deanne.
Deanne who?
I'm Deanne-sir to
your prayers!

Knock–knock.
Who's there?
Dee Wallace.
Dee wallace who?
"Dee Wallace came
tumbling down!"

Knock–knock.
    Who's there?
Deluxe.
    Deluxe who?
Deluxe Ness Monster.

Knock–knock.
    Who's there?
Demand.
    Demand who?
Demand from U.N.C.L.E.

Knock–knock.
    Who's there?
Denis.
    Denis who?
Denis anyone?

Knock–knock.
Who's there?
Dennis.
Dennis who?
Dennis says I've got a cavity.

Knock–knock.
Who's there?
Dennison.
Dennison who?
Dennison nice thing to say!

Knock–knock.
Who's there?
Denver.
Denver who?
Denver the good
old days.

Knock–knock.
Who's there?
Derision.
Derision who?
Derision room for
both of us in this town.

Knock–knock.
　Who's there?
Desi.
　Desi who?
Desi good reason why you think the world is against you–it is.

Knock–knock.
　Who's there?
Deuce.
　Deuce who?
Deuce something about your dog. He just bit me!

Knock–knock.
　Who's there?
Dexter.
　Dexter who?
"Dexter halls with boughs of holly . . ."

Knock–knock.
　Who's there?
D-1.
　D-1 who?
I'm D-1 to watch.

Knock–knock.
　Who's there?
Diane Kilburn.
　Diane Kilburn who?
"Diane Kilburn's (the ankle bone's) connected to the foot bone . . ."

D

Knock–knock.
    Who's there?
Diego.
    Diego who?
Diego all over your face—
what a sloppy eater!

Knock–knock.
    Who's there?
Diesel.
    Diesel who?
"Diesel man, he
played one, he
played nick-nack
on a drum . . ."

Knock–knock.
    Who's there?
Dion.
    Dion who?
Dion of thirst—can I
have a glass of water?

Knock–knock.
    Who's there?
Disease.
    Disease who?
Disease a disaster!

Knock–knock.
    Who's there?
Dishes.
    Dishes who?
Dishes the police—
open the door!

Knock–knock.
   Who's there?
Dishwasher.
   Dishwasher who?
Dishwasher last chance.

Knock–knock.
   Who's there?
Doberman pinscher.
   Doberman pinscher who?
Doberman pinscher and she
slugged him.

Knock–knock.
   Who's there?
Dizzy.
   Dizzy who?
Dizzy undertaker
know you're up?

Knock–knock.
   Who's there?
Dodson.
   Dodson who?
Dodson old Knock-Knock joke.

Knock–knock.
> Who's there?

Dog Catcher.
> Dog Catcher who?

Dog Catcher (don't count your) chickens before they hatch!

Knock–knock.
> Who's there?

Domino.
> Domino who?

"Domino thing if you don't have that swing . . ."

Knock–knock.
> Who's there?

Don Blaine.
> Don Blaine who?

Don Blaine (don't blame) me!

Knock–knock.
> Who's there?

Don.
> Don who?

Don mess around— just open the door.

Knock–knock.
  Who's there?
Don Boris Witty.
  Don Boris Witty who?
Don Boris Witty details!

Knock–knock.
  Who's there?
Don Juan.
  Don Juan who?
Don Juan to go out today?

Knock–knock.
  Who's there?
Don Marcus.
  Don Marcus who?
Don Marcus absent,
we're right here!

Knock–knock.
  Who's there?
Dona Lewis.
  Dona Lewis who?
Dona Lewis (don't lose)
your temper!

Knock–knock.
　Who's there?
Donahue.
　Donahue who?
Donahue hide from
me, you rat.

Knock–knock.
　Who's there?
Donald.
　Donald who?
Donald (don't hold)
your breath!

Knock–knock.
　Who's there?
Donat.
　Donat who?
Donat be so smart.
Remember, you can
always be replaced
by a human being.

Knock–knock.
　Who's there?
Donatello.
　Donatello who?
Donatello anybody,
but I'm a werewolf.

Knock–knock.
　Who's there?
Donovan.
　Donovan who?
Donovan think about it!

Knock–knock.
   Who's there?
Donna.
   Donna who?
"Way Donna-pon the
Swanee River . . ."

Knock–knock.
   Who's there?
Dora Belle.
   Dora Belle who?
Dora Belle is broken.
So I knocked.

Knock–knock.
   Who's there?
Donovan.
   Donovan who?
Donovan to hear another
word out of you.

Knock–knock.
Who's there?
Doris.
Doris who?
Doris no fool
like an old fool!

Knock–knock.
Who's there?
Dozer.
Dozer who?
Dozer the breaks.

Knock–knock.
Who's there?
Doughnut.
Doughnut who?
Doughnut be afraid—
it's only me!

D

Knock–knock.
    Who's there?
Dragon.
    Dragon who?
Dragon my name
through the mud?

Knock–knock.
    Who's there?
Dragon.
    Dragon who?
Quit Dragon
your tail!

Knock–knock.
    Who's there?
Dresden.
        Dresden who?
Dresden rags again?

Knock–knock.
 Who's there?
Dudes.
 Dudes who?
Dudes and don'ts.

Knock–knock.
 Who's there?
Duet.
 Duet who?
Duet right or don't
do it at all.

Knock–knock.
 Who's there?
Dunbar.
 Dunbar who?
Dunbar the door–I'll only
climb through the window.

Knock–knock.
 Who's there?
Duncan.
 Duncan who?
Duncan Donuts.

Knock–knock.
 Who's there?
Dutch.
 Dutch who?
Dutch me and I'll scream.

Knock-knock.
    Who's there?
Druscilla.
    Druscilla who?
Druscilla (drew a silly)
picture of the teacher.
    Knock-knock.
        Who's there?
Mamie.
        Mamie who?
She Mamie erase it.

    Knock-knock.
        Who's there?
Dwayne.
        Dwayne who?
"Dwayne in Spain falls mainly
in the plain . . ."
    Knock-knock.
        Who's there?
Wayne.
        Wayne who?
"Wayne, Wayne go away,
come again another day!"

Knock-Knock!

E
E
E

Knock–knock.
   Who's there?
Easter.
   Easter who?
Easter anybody home?

   Knock–knock.
      Who's there?
   Eaton.
      Eaton who?
   Eaton out of the
   garbage again?

Knock–knock.
Who's there?
Ed Rather.
Ed Rather who?
Ed Rather be sailing!

Knock–knock.
Who's there?
Edward B.
Edward B. who?
Edward B. nice if you
made like a bee and
buzzed off.

Knock–knock.
Who's there?
Efficient.
Efficient who?
Efficient my old pal!

Knock–knock.
    Who's there?
Effie.
    Effie who?
Effie-thing I have
is yours.

Knock–knock.
    Who's there?
Egypt.
    Egypt who?
Egypt you when he sold
you that busted doorbell.

Knock–knock.
Who's there?
Eiffel Tower.
Eiffel Tower who?
Eiffel (I feel) Towerable!

Knock–knock.
Who's there?
Elaine.
Elaine who?
Elaine down to take a nap.

Knock–knock.
Who's there?
Ma Belle.
Ma Belle who?
Ma Belle E. aches.

Knock–knock.
Who's there?
Cara Mia.
Cara Mia who?
Cara Mia to the doctor!

Knock–knock.
　Who's there?
Eiffel.
　Eiffel who?
Eiffel down and hurt
my knee.
　　Knock–knock.
　　Who's there?
Antony.
　　Antony who?
Antony still hurts.

Knock–knock.
　Who's there?
Eileen Dunn.
　Eileen Dunn who?
Eileen Dunn the bell
and it broke.

Knock–knock.
　Who's there?
Eisenhower.
　Eisenhower who?
Eisenhower late–sorry!

Knock–knock.
　Who's there?
Elia.
　Elia who?
Elia wake at night
thinking about you.

Knock–knock.
　Who's there?
Ella Mann.
　Ella Mann who?
Ella Mann-tary, my
dear Watson.

Knock–knock.
　Who's there?
Elke.
　Elke who?
"Elke seltzer . . .
Plop, plop,
fizz, fizz . . ."

Knock–knock.
　Who's there?
Ella.
　Ella who?
Ella-vator.
Doesn't that give
you a lift?

Knock–knock.
　Who's there?
Ellen.
　Ellen who?
Ellen-eed is love.

Knock–knock.
　Who's there?
Emma.
　Emma who?
Emma Nemms!

Knock–knock.
Who's there?
Emanuel.
Emanuel who?
Emanuel see turn into
a werewolf when the
moon is full.

Knock–knock.
Who's there?
Emma Lou King.
Emma Lou King who?
Emma Lou King into
my crystal ball . . .

Knock–knock.
Who's there?
Emerson.
Emerson who?
Emerson of a gun!

Knock–knock.
Who's there?
Emissary.
Emissary who?
Emissary I made you cry.

Knock–knock.
Who's there?
Encino.
Encino who?
Hear no evil, speak
no evil, Encino evil!

Knock–knock.
Who's there?
Enid Sue.
Enid Sue who?
Enid Sue like a hole
in the head!

Knock–knock.
Who's there?
Errol
Errol who?
Errol be a hot time in
the old town tonight!

Knock–knock.
Who's there?
Eskimo.
Eskimo who?
Eskimo questions–
I'll tell you no lies.

Knock–knock.
Who's there?
Estelle.
Estelle who?
Estelle am waiting
for you to open
this door!

Knock–knock.
Who's there?
Ethan.
Ethan who?
Ethan this the pits?

Knock–knock.
Who's there?
Etta.
Etta who?
Etta Boy!

Knock–knock.
Who's there?
Etta May Whit.
Etta May Whit who?
Etta May Whit- (At my wits')
send!

Knock–knock.
 Who's there?
Ether.
 Ether who?
Ether Bunny.

 Knock–knock.
  Who's there?
Cargo.
  Cargo who?
Cargo "beep-beep" and
run over Ether Bunny.

 Knock–knock.
  Who's there?
Stella.
   Stella who?
Stella 'nother Ether Bunny.

  Knock–knock.
   Who's there?
Consumption.
    Consumption who?
Consumption be done about
all these Ether Bunnies?

Knock–knock.
    Who's there?
Eubie.
    Eubie who?
Eubie-lieve in law and
order—if you lay down
the law and give the order.

Knock–knock.
    Who's there?
Eubie.
    Eubie who?
"Eubie long to me . . ."

Knock–knock.
    Who's there?
Eudora Belle.
    Eudora Belle who?
Eudora Belle thing, you!

Knock–knock.
    Who's there?
Eureka.
    Eureka who?
Eureka perfume! Who
sold it to you—a skunk?

Knock–knock.
    Who's there?
Eudora.
    Eudora who?
Eudora is stuck!

Knock–knock.
    Who's there?
Europe.
    Europe who?
Europe (you're up)
to no good!

Knock–knock.
    Who's there?
European.
    European who?
European in the
neck.

Knock–knock.
    Who's there?
Evan.
    Evan who?
Evan Lee coffee!

Knock–knock.
    Who's there?
Evan.
    Evan who?
Evan seen
anything like you
since the Rocky
Horror Show.

Knock–knock.
    Who's there?
Eye Sore.
    Eye Sore who?
Eye Sore them coming!

Knock–knock.
    Who's there?
Ewell.
    Ewell who?
Ewell catch more flies
with honey than with
vinegar!

Knock–knock.

Who's there?

Eyes.

Eyes who?

Eyes got another
Knock-Knock joke.

Knock–knock.

Who's there?

Nose.

Nose who?

I nose another
Knock-Knock joke.

Knock–knock.

Who's there?

Ears.

Ears who?

Ears another
Knock-Knock joke.

Knock–knock.

Who's there?

Chin.

Chin who?

Chin up—I'm not going to
tell any more Knock-Knock
jokes.

Knock-Knock!

F

Knock–knock.
   Who's there?
F-2.
   F-2 who?
Do I F-2 tell you?

Knock–knock.
   Who's there?
Fallacy.
   Fallacy who?
I Fallacy (fail to see)
what's so funny!

Knock–knock.
   Who's there?
Fanny.
   Fanny who?
Fanny body calls,
I'm out.

Knock–knock.
   Who's there?
Fanny.
   Fanny who?
Fanny you should ask!

Knock–knock.
   Who's there?
Far Side.
   Far Side who?
As Far Side (far as I)
know, it's still me!

Knock–knock.
   Who's there?
Faraday.
   Faraday who?
Faraday last time,
open up!

Knock–knock.
   Who's there?
Farrah.
   Farrah who?
Farrah 'n wide.

Knock–knock.
   Who's there?
Farrah.
   Farrah who?
Farrah out, man.

Knock–knock.
   Who's there?
Farris.
   Farris who?
"Mirror, mirror on
the wall. Who's the
Farris one of all?"

Knock–knock.
   Who's there?
Father.
   Father who?
The Father the better!

Knock–knock.
   Who's there?
Fatso Kay.
   Fatso Kay who?
Fatso Kay with you,
Fatso Kay with me!

Knock–knock.
    Who's there?
Fedora.
    Fedora who?
Fedora shut, does that
mean I can't come in?

Knock–knock.
    Who's there?
Ferdie.
    Ferdie who?
Ferdie last time,
open the door!

Knock–knock.
    Who's there?
Ferrara.
    Ferrara who?
"Long ago and
Ferrara-way . . ."

Knock–knock.
    Who's there?
Ferris.
    Ferris who?
Ferris I'm concerned,
we're through.

Knock–knock.
    Who's there?
Felix.
    Felix who?
Felix-cited all over.

Knock–knock.
    Who's there?
Fess.
    Fess who?
Fess Aid Squad.

Knock–knock.
    Who's there?
Fiddlesticks.
    Fiddlesticks who?
Fiddlesticks (feet'll stick) out
if the blanket's too short.

Knock–knock.
    Who's there?
Fidel.
    Fidel who?
Fidel you a secret, will
you keep it to yourself?

Knock–knock.
    Who's there?
Fido.
    Fido who?
Fido away, what
will you give me?

Knock–knock.
    Who's there?
Fiendish.
    Fiendish who?
Fiendish your dinner!

Knock–knock.
    Who's there?
Fiona.
(Pronounced Fee-oh-na)
    Fiona who?
Fiona had something better
to do, do you think we'd
hang around here?

Knock–knock.
    Who's there?
Fission.
    Fission who?
Fission for compliments!

F

Knock–knock.
　　Who's there?
Fitzhugh.
　　Fitzhugh who?
If the shoe Fitzhugh
wear it!

Knock–knock.
　　Who's there?
Fletcher.
　　Fletcher who?
Fletcher self go!

Knock–knock.
　　Who's there?
Flaherty.
　　Flaherty who?
Flaherty will get
you nowhere!

Knock–knock.
Who's there?
Fonzi.
Fonzi who?
Fonzi meeting
you here!

Knock–knock.
Who's there?
Florist.
Florist who?
You can't see the
Florist for the trees!

Knock–knock.
Who's there?
Ford.
Ford who?
Ford-y thieves.

Knock–knock.
Who's there?
Foreign.
Foreign who?
"Foreign twenty
blackbirds baked
in a pie . . ."

Knock–knock.
Who's there?
Formosa.
Formosa who?
Formosa my life, I've
been waiting for you
to open the door!

Knock–knock.
Who's there?
Formosa.
Formosa who?
Formosa the day
I've had my foot stuck
in this door.

Knock–knock.
Who's there?
Forty.
Forty who?
Forty last time,
open up!

Knock–knock.
　Who's there?
Frank.
　Frank who?
Frank N. Stein. Aaggh!

Knock–knock.
　Who's there?
Frank's eye.
　Frank's eye who?
Frank's eye needed that.

Knock–knock.
　Who's there?
Franz.
　Franz who?
"Franz, Romans, countrymen . . ."

Knock–knock.
　Who's there?
Frank Lee.
　Frank Lee who?
Frank Lee, it's none of
your business.

Knock–knock.
　Who's there?
Franz.
　Franz who?
Franz forever!

Knock–knock.
Who's there?
Fred.
Fred who?
Fred I'll have to tell
you another joke.

Knock–knock.
Who's there?
Freddie.
Freddie who?
Freddie or not, here
I come.

Knock–knock.
Who's there?
Freedom.
Freedom who?
Never mind—let
freedom ring.

Knock–knock.
Who's there?
Free Stew.
Free Stew who?
The Free Stew-ges
(The Three Stooges).

Knock–knock.
Who's there?
Freeze.
Freeze who?
"Freeze a jolly
good fellow . . ."

Knock–knock.
　Who's there?
Freighter.
　　Freighter who?
Freighter open the door?

Knock–knock.
　Who's there?
Freud.
　　Freud who?
A-Freud you were
going to ask that.

Knock–knock.
　Who's there?
Fresno.
　　Fresno who?
"Rudolf the Fresno
reindeer . . ."

Knock–knock.
　Who's there?
Fu Manchu.
　　Fu Manchu who?
Fu Manchu bubble gum
the way you do.

Knock–knock.
　Who's there?
Frieda.
　　Frieda who?
Who's a Frieda the
big bad wolf?

Knock-Knock!

G

Knock–knock.
> Who's there?

GM.
> GM who?

GM I rattling your cage?

91

Knock–knock.
   Who's there?
Gallo.
   Gallo who?
Gallo your dreams.

Knock–knock.
   Who's there?
Galahad.
   Galahad who?
I knew a Galahad
two left feet!

Knock–knock.
   Who's there?
Garcia.
   Garcia who?
Garcia (go see) the
principal.

Knock–knock.
   Who's there?
Garter.
      Garter who?
Garter go now!

Knock–knock.
   Who's there?
Gauguin.
   Gauguin who?
Gauguin, it's your turn!

Knock–knock.
   Who's there?
Ghana.
   Ghana who?
Not Ghana take this
anymore.

Knock–knock.
Who's there?
Gavin.
Gavin who?
Gavin you one more chance
to open the door!

Knock–knock.
Who's there?
Dustin.
Dustin who?
Dustin off the battering ram!

Knock–knock.
Who's there?
Germaine.
Germaine who?
Germaine (you're mean)
to act this way!

Knock–knock.
Who's there?
Gideon.
Gideon who?
Gideon your horse
and let's go!

Knock–knock.
Who's there?
Gillette.
Gillette who?
If Gillette me in, I
won't knock anymore.

Knock–knock.
Who's there?
Giovanni.
Giovanni who?
Giovanni come out and play?

Knock–knock.
Who's there?
Festival.
Festival who?
Festival I have to do my homework.

Knock–knock.
Who's there?
Gibbon.
Gibbon who?
Are you Gibbon me trouble?

Knock–knock.
Who's there?
Gil Diaz.
Gil Diaz who?
Gil Diaz (guilty as) charged!

Knock–knock.
Who's there?
Giuseppe.
Giuseppe who?
Giuseppe (just stepped) in something on your doorstep.

Knock–knock.
Who's there?
Houdini.
Houdini who?
Houdini that thing on your doorstep?

Knock–knock.
Who's there?
Gladwin.
Gladwin who?
Gladwin you leave town.

Knock–knock.
Who's there?
Gladys.
Gladys who?
Gladys see you.

Knock–knock.
Who's there?
G-Man.
G-Man who?
G-Man-y Crickets!

Knock–knock.
Who's there?
Goody.
Goody who?
"Goody-vening!" says
Count Dracula.

Knock–knock.
Who's there?
Venom.
Venom who?
Venom I going to get inside?

Knock-knock.
 Who's there?
Goat.
 Goat who?
Goat to your room!

Knock–knock.
 Who's there?
Goddess.
 Goddess who?
Goddess stop meeting
like this.

Knock–knock.
 Who's there?
Goddard.
 Goddard who?
You Goddard be kidding!

Knock–knock.
 Who's there?
Aikido.
 Aikido who?
Aikido you not!

Knock–knock.
   Who's there?
Gopher.
   Gopher who?
Gopher (go for) broke.

Knock–knock.
   Who's there?
Gorilla.
   Gorilla who?
Gorilla cheese sandwich.

Knock–knock.
   Who's there?
Gray Z.
   Gray Z. who?
Gray Z. mixed-up kid!

Knock–knock.
   Who's there?
Goliath.
   Goliath who?
Goliath down. You're
sick in the head.

Knock–knock.
   Who's there?
Gordie.
   Gordie who?
Gordie-rectly to jail.
Do not pass Go.
Do not collect $200.

Knock–knock.
   Who's there?
Grammar.
   Grammar who?
Grammar crackers.
Pretty crummy, huh?

Knock–knock.
   Who's there?
Greta.
   Greta who?
You Greta my nerves.

Knock–knock.
Who's there?
Gretel.
Gretel who?
"Gretel-long little dogie . . ."

Knock–knock.
Who's there?
Guava.
Guava who?
Guava good time!

Knock–knock.
Who's there?
Gucci.
Gucci who?
Gucci-Gucci-Goo!

Knock–knock.
Who's there?
Guinevere.
Guinevere who?
Guinevere going to get together?

Knock–knock.
Who's there?
Guinness.
Guinness who?
Guinness a break!

Knock–knock.
Who's there?
Gunboat.
Gunboat who?
You're Gunboat not forgotten.

Knock–knock.
　Who's there?
Gummy.
　Gummy who?
Gummy five!

Knock–knock.
　Who's there?
Gus.
　Gus who?
That's what *you're*
supposed to do.

Knock–knock.
　Who's there?
Gunnar.
　Gunnar who?
Gunnar huff and puff
and blow your house in.

Knock–knock.
　Who's there?
Guthrie.
　Guthrie who?
Guthrie blind mice.

Knock–knock.
　Who's there?
Gwynn N.
　Gwynn N. who?
Gwynn N. bear it!

Knock-Knock!

Knock–knock.
> Who's there?

Habit.
> Habit who?

Habit your own way!

Knock–knock.
> Who's there?

Hackett.
> Hackett who?

I can't Hackett—
I'm going home.

Knock–knock.
> Who's there?

Haiku.
> Haiku who?

"Haiku-d have danced
all night . . ."

Knock–knock.
    Who's there?
Hair combs.
    Hair combs who?
Hair Combs the judge!

Knock–knock.
    Who's there?
Halibut.
    Halibut who?
Halibut lending me
five dollars?

Knock–knock.
    Who's there?
Hallways.
    Hallways who?
Hallways knew you'd
never amount to much.

Customer:	**Knock–knock.**
Waiter:	Who's there?
Customer:	Hammond.
Waiter:	Hammond who?
Customer:	Hammond eggs, please.

Knock–knock.
> Who's there?

Hannah.
> Hannah who?

"Hannah partridge
in a pear tree . . ."

Knock–knock.
> Who's there?

Hanover.
> Hanover who?

Hanover your money.

Knock-knock.
Who's there?
Hans.
Hans who?
Hans up! I'm a burglar.
Knock–knock.
Who's there?
Jimmy.
Jimmy who?
Jimmy your money–or else!
Knock–knock.
Who's there?
Bruce.
Bruce who?
Careful–I Bruce easily.

Knock–knock.
Who's there?
Hardy.
Hardy who?
Hardy, har, har!

Knock–knock.
Who's there?
Harley.
Harley who?
Harley ever see you
around anymore.

Knock–knock.
Who's there?
Harmon.
Harmon who?
Harmon your side.

Knock–knock.
  Who's there?
Harmony.
  Harmony who?
Harmony times do I have
to knock at this door?

Knock–knock.
  Who's there?
Harold.
  Harold who?
Harold are you?

Knock–knock.
  Who's there?
Harris.
  Harris who?
Harris the world treating you?

H

Knock–knock.
  Who's there?
Harrison.
  Harrison who?
Harrison idea–you tell the next
joke!

Knock–knock.
  Who's there?
Hartley.
  Hartley who?
This is Hartley the time to be
telling knock-knock jokes!

Knock–knock.
　Who's there?
Harv and Hugh.
　Harv and Hugh who?
Harv and Hugh (haven't you)
got a minute?

Knock–knock.
　Who's there?
Harvey.
　Harvey who?
Harvey going to play
this game forever?

Knock–knock.
　Who's there?
Healy.
　Healy who?
Healy my pain . . .

Knock–knock.
　Who's there?
Harvard.
　Harvard who?
Harvard you like a
punch in the nose?

Knock–knock.
　Who's there?
Hattie.
　Hattie who?
Hattie do, you all!

Knock–knock.
　Who's there?
Hawaii.
　Hawaii who?
Hawaii doing?

Knock–knock.
　Who's there?
Heath.
　Heath who?
"For Heath a jolly
good fellow . . ."

Knock–knock.
    Who's there?
Heaven.
    Heaven who?
Heaven seen you
for a long time.

Knock–knock.
    Who's there?
Hedda.
    Hedda who?
Hedda I win, tails
you lose!

Knock–knock.
    Who's there?
Heidi.
    Heidi who?
Heidi go seek.

Knock–knock.
    Who's there?
Hedda.
    Hedda who?
Hedda feeling you
wouldn't open the
door.

Knock–knock.
    Who's there?
Heide.
    Heide who?
Heide-clare war on you!

Knock–knock.
    Who's there?
Heifer.
    Heifer who?
Heifer (half a) cow
is better than none.

Knock–knock.
    Who's there?
Hello Etta.
    Hello Etta who?
"Hello Etta, gentille Alouetta . . ."

107

Knock–knock.
  Who's there?
Henny.
  Henny who?
Henny Penny. The sky
is falling down!
  Knock–knock.
    Who's there?
Izzy.
    Izzy who?
Izzy end of the world!

Knock–knock.
  Who's there?
Henrietta.
  Henrietta who?
Henrietta big dinner and
got sick.
  Knock–knock.
    Who's there?
Romeo and Juliet.
    Romeo and Juliet who?
Romeo and Juliet the same
thing–and died.

Knock–knock.
Who's there?
Hester.
Hester who?
Hester any food left?
Knock–knock.
Who's there?
Pasadena.
Pasadena who?
Pasadena under the door–I'm starved.

Knock–knock.
　　Who's there?
Hertz.
　　Hertz who?
Hertz me more than it hurts you.

Knock–knock.
　　Who's there?
Hewlett.
　　Hewlett who?
Hewlett you out of your cage?

Knock–knock.
　　Who's there?
Heywood, Hugh and Harry.
　　Heywood, Hugh and Harry who?
Heywood, Hugh Harry and open the door!

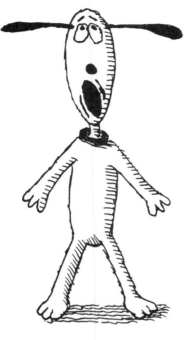

Knock–knock.
Who's there?
Hiawatha.
Hiawatha who?
Hiawatha very bad today.

Knock–knock.
Who's there?
Highway cop.
Highway cop who?
Highway cop screaming–
thinking of you.

Knock–knock.
Who's there?
Hiram.
Hiram who?
Hiram fine, how are you?

Knock–knock.
Who's there?
Hiram.
Hiram who?
Hiram glad you asked!

Knock–knock.
　Who's there?
Hobbit.
　Hobbit who?
Hobbit letting me in?

Knock–knock.
　Who's there?
Holden.
　Holden who?
Holden up everything
on account of you.

Knock–knock.
　Who's there?
Hollis.
　Hollis who?
Come back, Hollis
(all is) forgiven!

Knock–knock.
　Who's there?
Hominy.
　Hominy who?
Hominy rocks did they
have to turn up before
you crawled out?

Knock–knock.
　Who's there?
Holmes.
　Holmes who?
Holmes sweet home.

Knock–knock.
　Who's there?
Honda.
　Honda who?
"Home, home Honda
range . . ."

Knock–knock.
　Who's there?
Honda.
　Honda who?
Honda road again!

Knock–knock.
　Who's there?
Honorless.
　Honorless who?
Honorless you open this door,
I'll have to break it down!

Knock–knock.
　Who's there?
Horace.
　Horace who?
Horace of a different color!

Knock–knock.
　Who's there?
Honeydew.
　Honeydew who?
Honeydew you think you're
ever going to open the door?

Knock–knock.
　Who's there?
Horace.
　Horace who?
Horace I to know
you lived here?

Knock–knock.
　Who's there?
House.
　House who?
House it going?

Knock–knock.
Who's there?
Hoodoo.
Hoodoo who?
Hoodoo you want it to be?

Knock–knock.
Who's there?
San Juan.
San Juan who?
San Juan (someone) else!

Knock–knock.
Who's there?
Howard.
Howard who?
Howard I know?

Knock–knock.
Who's there?
Howard.
Howard who?
Howard you like to crawl back under your rock?

Knock–knock.
Who's there?
Howell.
Howell who?
Howell I get in if you don't answer the door?

H

Knock–knock.
Who's there?
Hubie Maddern.
Hubie Maddern who?
Hubie Maddern a wet hen!

Knock–knock.
Who's there?
Hugh Hefner.
Hugh Hefner who?
Hugh Hefner trouble with
the doorknob again?

Knock–knock.
Who's there?
Hugo N.
Hugo N. who?
Hugo N. Crazy–
and I'm goin' home.

Knock–knock.
Who's there?
Humus.
Humus who?
Humus be sick–that
can't be your real face!

Tap–tap.
Who's there?
Hurd.
Hurd who?
Hurd my hand so I
can't knock-knock.

Knock–knock.
    Who's there?
Hutch.
    Hutch who?
Gersundheit!

Knock–knock.
    Who's there?
Huron.
    Huron who?
Huron away from
home again?

H

Knock–knock.
    Who's there?
Hy.
    Hy who?
Hy-oh, Silver!

Knock–knock.
    Who's there?
Hyam Alda.
    Hyam Alda who?
Hyam Alda washed up.

Knock-Knock!

Knock–knock.
　Who's there?
I.B. Long.
　I.B. Long who?
I.B. Long inside.
It's cold out here.

Knock–knock.
　Who's there?
Ice Water.
　Ice Water who?
My Ice Water when I
chop onions!

Knock–knock.
Who's there?
Ice cream soda.
Ice cream soda who?
Ice cream soda (I scream so the) whole world will know what a nut you are.

Knock–knock.
Who's there?
Ichabod.
Ichabod who?
Ichabod (it's a bad) night out. Can I borrow your umbrella?

Knock–knock.
Who's there?
Icon.
Icon who?
Icon live without you!

Knock–knock.
Who's there?
Ida Clair.
Ida Clair who?
Ida Clair, you're the most stubborn person!

Knock–knock.
Who's there?
Ida Klein.
Ida Klein who?
Ida Klein to answer that question!

Knock–knock.
Who's there?
Ida.
Ida who?
Ida know. Sorry.

Knock–knock.
Who's there?
Ida.
Ida who?
Idaho–not Ida-who!
Can't you spell?

Knock–knock.
Who's there?
Igloo.
Igloo who?
"Igloo knew Suzie
like I know Suzie . . ."

Knock–knock.
Who's there?
Igor.
Igor who?
Igor to see you again.

Knock–knock.
Who's there?
India.
India who?
"India good old
summertime . . ."

Knock–knock.
Who's there?
Ina Claire.
Ina Claire who?
"Ina Claire day, you
can see forever . . ."

Knock–knock.
   Who's there?
Indonesia.
   Indonesia who?
I look at you and I get weak Indonesia.

Knock–knock.
   Who's there?
Indochina.
   Indochina who?
The bull Indochina shop.

Knock–knock.
Who's there?
Iodine.
Iodine who?
Iodine (I'm a dyin')
for a pizza!

Knock–knock.
Who's there?
Iona.
Iona who?
"Iona have one life to
give for my country . . ."

Knock–knock.
Who's there?
I-one.
I-one who?
"I-one-der who's
kissing her now . . ."

Knock–knock.
Who's there?
Iona.
Iona who?
"Iona have eyes
for you . . ."

Knock–knock.
Who's there?
Iris.
Iris who?
Iris you were here.

Knock–knock.
Who's there?
Ira.
Ira who?
Ira-turn with another
Knock-knock joke.

Knock–knock.
  Who's there?
Iris.
  Iris who?
Iris you were here.

Knock–knock.
  Who's there?
Iraq and Iran.
  Iraq and Iran who?
Iraq'd up the car and
Iran all the way over.

Knock–knock.
  Who's there?
Irish Stew.
  Irish Stew who?
Irish Stew would come
out and play.

Knock–knock.
  Who's there?
Isabelle.
  Isabelle who?
Isabelle broken?

Knock–knock.
  Who's there?
Isadore.
  Isadore who?
Isadore stuck?

Knock–knock.
  Who's there?
Isaiah.
  Isaiah who?
Isaiah there, old chap, why
don't you open the door?

Knock–knock.
  Who's there?
Istanbul.
  Istanbul who?
Istanbul fight over?

Knock–knock.
  Who's there?
Isthmus.
  Isthmus who?
Isthmus be the right place.

Knock–knock.
    Who's there?
Ivan.
    Ivan who?
Ivan infectious disease.

Knock–knock.
    Who's there?
Ivy Leaf.
    Ivy Leaf who?
Ivy Leaf you alone.

Knock–knock.
    Who's there?
Ivan.
    Ivan who?
"Ivan working on
the railroad . . ."

Knock-Knock!

Knock–knock.
Who's there?
Jack N.
Jack N. who?
Jack N. the Box.

Knock–knock.
Who's there?
Janet R.
Janet R. who?
Janet R. in a drum.

Knock–knock.
Who's there?
Java.
Java who?
Java lot to learn!

Knock–knock.
Who's there?
Jackal.
Jackal who?
Jackal lantern.

Knock–knock.
Who's there?
Jeff.
Jeff who?
Jeff Boy-R-Dee.

Knock–knock.
    Who's there?
Jenny.
    Jenny who?
Jenny'd any help
opening the door?

Knock–knock.
    Who's there?
Jerome.
    Jerome who?
Have it Jerome way!

Knock–knock.
    Who's there?
Jess Horace.
    Jess Horace who?
Jess Horace-n' around!

Knock–knock.
    Who's there?
Jericho.
    Jericho who?
Jericho to Disneyland?

Knock–knock.
    Who's there?
Jess B.
    Jess B. who?
Jess B. Cuzz!

Knock–knock.
    Who's there?
Jess.
    Jess who?
Jess knock it off!

Knock–knock.
    Who's there?
Jess me.
    Jess me who?
"Jess me and my
shadow . . ."

126

Knock–knock.
Who's there?
Jess.
Jess who?
Jess one of those things.

Knock–knock.
Who's there?
Jason.
Jason who?
"I'm always Jason
rainbows . . ."

Knock–knock.
Who's there?
Jessica.
Jessica who?
Jessica (you're sicker)
than I thought.

Knock–knock.
Who's there?
Jester.
Jester who?
Jester minute, pardner.

Knock–knock.
Who's there?
Jester.
Jester who?
Jester minute, I've got
more knock-knock jokes!

Knock–knock.
    Who's there?
Jethro.
    Jethro who?
Jethro (just throw)
me a few bones.

Knock–knock.
    Who's there?
Jethro.
    Jethro who?
Jethro the boat and
stop talking so much.

Knock–knock.
    Who's there?
Jezebel.
    Jezebel who?
Jezebel on the door,
but it won't ring.

Knock–knock.
    Who's there?
Jewel.
    Jewel who?
Jewel (you'll) remember me
after you see my face.

Knock–knock.
    Who's there?
Joe King.
    Joe King who?
You must be Joe King!

Knock–knock.
Who's there?
Jock.
Jock who?
Jock-late milk shake.

Knock–knock.
Who's there?
Johann Sebastian Bach.
Johann Sebastian Bach who?
Johann Sebastian Bach in town!

Knock–knock.
Who's there?
John Q.
John Q. who?
John Q. very much.

Knock–knock.
Who's there?
Juan.
Juan who?
Juan good turn
deserves another!

Knock–knock.
Who's there?
Juana.
Juana who?
Juana improve your
looks? Wear a mask.

Knock–knock.
    Who's there?
Juan.
    Juan who?
Juan two, buckle my shoe . . .

    Knock–knock.
        Who's there?
Grigor.
    Grigor who?
Grigor (three, four),
shut the door . . .

        Knock–knock.
        Who's there?
Physics.
        Physics who?
Physics (five, six),
pick up sticks.

        Knock–knock.
        Who's there?
Stefan Haight.
        Stefan Haight who?
Stefan Haight, lay them
straight.

Knock–knock.
Who's there?
Juarez.
Juarez who?
Juarez you hiding,
you rascal you?

Knock–knock.
Who's there?
Jubilee.
Jubilee who?
Jubilee-ve in the
tooth fairy?

Knock–knock.
Who's there?
Judah.
Judah who?
Judah known by now if
you opened the door.

Knock–knock.
Who's there?
Juicy Watt.
Juicy Watt who?
Juicy Watt someone
wrote on your door?

Knock–knock.
  Who's there?
Juneau.
  Juneau who?
Juneau what time it is?
    Knock–knock.
      Who's there?
Nome.
      Nome who?
Nome, I don't.
      Knock–knock.
        Who's there?
Alaska.
        Alaska who?
Alaska someone else.

Knock–knock.
  Who's there?
Jupiter.
    Jupiter who?
Jupiter hurry or
you'll miss the
garbage truck.

Knock–knock.
  Who's there?
Justin.
    Justin who?
Justin time for dinner.

Knock–knock.
  Who's there?
Justine.
    Justine who?
Justine old fashioned girl.

Knock–knock.
  Who's there?
Justis.
    Justis who?
Justis I thought.
Wrong door.

Knock-Knock!

Knock–knock.
  Who's there?
Kareem Cohen.
  Kareem Cohen who?
Ice Kareem Cohen!

Knock–knock.
  Who's there?
Keefe.
  Keefe who?
Keefe me one
more chance!

Knock–knock.
  Who's there?
Karen.
  Karen who?
Karen-teed to crack
you up!

Knock–knock.
   Who's there?
Keith.
   Keith who?
Keith me, you fool!

Knock–knock.
   Who's there?
Ken D.
   Ken D. who?
Ken D. Gram.

Knock–knock.
   Who's there?
Ken.
   Ken who?
Ken I come in?
It's freezing out here.

Knock–knock.
   Who's there?
Kenya.
   Kenya who?
Kenya hear me
knocking? I said
"Knock-Knock!"

Knock–knock.
   Who's there?
Kenya.
   Kenya who?
Kenya keep it
down in there?

Knock–knock.
　Who's there?
Ketchup.
　Ketchup who?
Ketchup with me and
I'll tell you.

Knock–knock.
　Who's there?
Kevin.
　Kevin who?
"Thank Kevin for little girls . . ."

Knock–knock.
　Who's there?
Kiefer.
　Kiefer who?
Kiefer stiff upper lip.

Knock–knock.
　Who's there?
Kimono.
　Kimono who?
Kimono my house.

Knock–knock.
　Who's there?
King Kong.
　King Kong who?
"King Kong, the witch
is dead . . ."

Knock–knock.
　Who's there?
Kip.
　Kip who?
Kip talking. Maybe
you'll find something
to say.

Knock–knock.
　Who's there?
Kipper.
　Kipper who?
Kipper hands to
yourself.

Knock-knock.
Who's there?
Klaus.
Klaus who?
Klaus your mouth
and open the door!

Knock-knock.
Who's there?
Koala.
Koala who?
Koala-T jokes like these
are hard to find.

Knock-knock.
Who's there?
Kojak.
Kojak who?
Kojak up the car.
We've got a flat.

Knock-knock.
Who's there?
Krakatoa.
Krakatoa who?
Just Krakatoa trying to
kick this door down!

Knock-knock.
Who's there?
Kris.
Kris who?
Kris P. Critters!

K

Knock–knock.
Who's there?
Kumquat.
Kumquat who?
Kumquat may, we'll
always be buddies.

Knock–knock.
Who's there?
Kurt.
Kurt who?
Kurt that out!

Knock–knock.
Who's there?
Kurt and Conan.
Kurt and Cohan who?
Kurt and Conan (curtain coming)
down on the last act.

Knock-Knock!

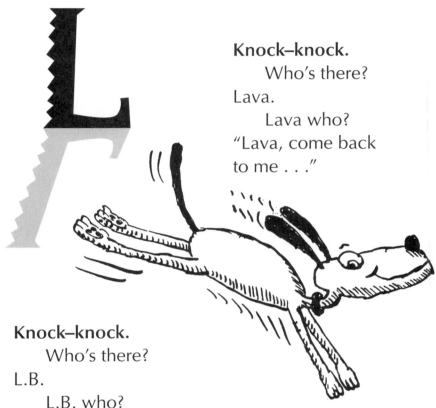

Knock–knock.
　Who's there?
Lava.
　Lava who?
"Lava, come back
to me . . ."

Knock–knock.
　Who's there?
L.B.
　L.B. who?
L.B. the judge of that!

Knock–knock.
　Who's there?
Lee King.
　Lee King who?
Lee King bucket.

Knock–knock.
　Who's there?
Leah Penn.
　Leah Penn who?
Leah Penn Lizards!

L

Knock–knock.
   Who's there?
Lemuel.
   Lemuel who?
Lemuel kicked me.

Knock–knock.
   Who's there?
Thor.
   Thor who?
Thor all over.

Knock–knock.
   Who's there?
Lester.
   Lester who?
Lester the Red Hot
Mamas.

Knock–knock.
   Who's there?
Lettuce.
   Lettuce who?
Lettuce in and we'll
tell you another
Knock-Knock joke.

Knock–knock.
   Who's there?
Leonie.
   Leonie who?
Leonie thing you
do fast is get tired.

Knock–knock.
   Who's there?
Lettuce.
   Lettuce who?
Lettuce discuss this
like mature adults . . .

Knock–knock.
Who's there?
Lima bean.
Lima bean who?
"Lima bean (I've been)
working on the railroad . . ."

Knock–knock.
Who's there?
Linda.
Linda who?
Linda helping hand.
Knock–knock.
Who's there?
Yukon.
Yukon who?
Yukon count on me.

Knock–knock.
Who's there?
Lion.
Lion who?
Lion here on your doorstep
till you open the door.

Knock–knock.
　Who's there?
Lionel.
　Lionel who?
Lionel bite you if you
don't watch out.

Knock–knock.
　Who's there?
Lion.
　Lion who?
Lion down on the
job again?

Knock–knock.
　Who's there?
Lionel.
　Lionel who?
Lionel get you in
trouble!

Knock–knock.
　Who's there?
Lisa.
　Lisa who?
Lisa you can do
is let me in.

Knock–knock.
　Who's there?
Little old lady.
　Little old lady who?
I didn't know you could yodel.

L

Knock–knock.
    Who's there?
Lucas Tell.
    Lucas Tell who?
Lucas Tell-oh and
Bud Abbott.

Knock–knock.
    Who's there?
Lotto.
    Lotto who?
Lotto trouble coming
your way if you don't
open up.

Knock–knock.
    Who's there?
Lucinda.
    Lucinda who?
Lucinda chain and
let me inside.

L

Knock–knock.
Who's there?
Lucretia.
Lucretia who?
Lucretia (the creature)
from the Black Lagoon.

Knock–knock.
Who's there?
Lucy.
Lucy who?
Lucy Nupp!

Knock–knock.
Who's there?
Lufthansa.
Lufthansa who?
Lufthansa! This is a
stick-up!

144

Knock–knock.
 Who's there?
Luigi.
 Luigi who?
Luigi board.

Knock–knock.
 Who's there?
Luke.
 Luke who?
Luke before you leap.

Knock–knock.
 Who's there?
Luke.
 Luke who?
Luke through the
keyhole and see.

Knock–knock.
 Who's there?
Luke.
 Luke who?
Luke out below!

Knock–knock.
Who's there?
Lyle.
Lyle who?
Lyle be a monkey's
uncle!

Knock–knock.
Who's there?
Lyndon.
Lyndon who?
Lyndon ear and
I'll tell you.

Knock-Knock!

Scratch–scratch.
Who's there?
M-2.
M-2 who?
M-2 weak to knock.

Knock–knock.
Who's there?
Mabel.
Mabel who?
Mabel I'll tell you
and Mabel I won't!

Knock–knock.
Who's there?
Mack.
Mack who?
Mack up your mind!

Knock–knock.
Who's there?
Madge.
Madge who?
Madge N. that!

Knock–knock.
Who's there?
Madison.
Madison who?
You're Madison hatter!

Knock–knock.
    Who's there?
Ma Harrison.
    Ma Harrison who?
Ma Harrison (my hair is on) fire!

Knock–knock.
    Who's there?
Mamie.
    Mamie who?
The Devil Mamie
do it!

Knock–knock.
    Who's there?
Mandy.
    Mandy who?
Mandy lifeboats!
The ship is sinking!

Knock–knock.
    Who's there?
Mannheim.
    Mannheim who?
Mannheim tired!

M

Knock–knock.
Who's there?
Manny Dunn.
Manny Dunn who?
Manny Dunn grow on trees.

Knock–knock.
Who's there?
Mansion.
Mansion who?
Did I Mansion I have
more knock-knock jokes?

M

Knock–knock.
Who's there?
Marmoset.
Marmoset who?
Marmoset there'd be
days like this.

Knock–knock.
Who's there?
Marsha.
Marsha who?
Marsha Mallow!

Knock–knock.
Who's there?
Mary and Abbey.
Mary and Abbey who?
Mary Christmas and Abbey
New Year!

Knock–knock.
Who's there?
Maude.
Maude who?
Maude as well go home.

Knock–knock.
Who's there?
Mavis.
Mavis who?
Mavis be the last time
I knock at your door.

Knock–knock.
Who's there?
Math.
Math who?
Math (mashed)
Potatoes!

Knock–knock.
Who's there?
May Kay.
May Kay who?
May Kay while the
sun shines!

Knock–knock.
Who's there?
Maynard.
Maynard who?
Maynard come
around anymore
if you don't open up.

Knock–knock.
Who's there?
Mayonnaise.
Mayonnaise who?
"Mayonnaise have seen
the glory of the coming
of the Lord . . ."

Knock–knock.
Who's there?
Mazda.
Mazda who?
Mazda of the
Universe!

Knock–knock.
Who's there?
Megan.
Megan who?
Megan a phone call.

Knock–knock.
Who's there?
Jessamyn.
Jessamyn who?
Jessamyn-it please–
the lion is busy.

Knock–knock.
Who's there?
Mustang.
Mustang who?
Mustang up now–
I'm out of change.

Knock–knock.
Who's there?
Megan, Elise and Chicken.
Megan, Elise and Chicken who?
"He's Megan, Elise and Chicken it twice,
gonna find out who's naughty and nice . . ."

Knock–knock.
Who's there?
Meteor.
Meteor who?
Prepare to Meteor
(meet your) maker!

Knock–knock.
Who's there?
Melissa.
Melissa who?
Melissa to you and
I get in trouble.

Knock–knock.
Who's there?
Michael Rhoda.
Michael Rhoda who?
"Michael Rhoda boat ashore,
hallelujah . . ."

Knock–knock.
Who's there?
Midas.
Midas who?
Midas well try again—
knock-knock!

Knock–knock.
Who's there?
Mimi.
Mimi who?
Mimi at the pool. I'd like to
give you drowning lessons.

Knock–knock.
Who's there?
Meyer.
Meyer who?
Meyer in a nasty
mood!

Knock–knock.
Who's there?
Midas.
Midas who?
Midas well relax. I'm
not going any place.

Knock–knock.
Who's there?
Mike Rowe.
Mike Rowe who?
Mike Rowe wave oven.

Knock–knock.
   Who's there?
Mike Howe.
   Mike Howe who?
Mike Howe is sick.

   Knock–knock.
     Who's there?
Yvette.
     Yvette who?
Yvette fixed her up.

M

Knock–knock.
Who's there?
Mindy.
Mindy who?
Mindy mood for pizza.

Knock–knock.
Who's there?
Nova.
Nova who?
Nova good place for pizza?

Knock–knock.
Who's there?
Noah.
Noah who?
Noah don't.

Knock–knock.
Who's there?
Newton.
Newton who?
Newton Monday,
but I forgot.

Knock–knock.
   Who's there?
Minerva.
   Minerva who?
Minerva-s wreck from
all these questions.

Knock–knock.
   Who's there?
Minna.
   Minna who?
Minna wrong place
at the wrong time.

Knock–knock.
   Who's there?
Minneapolis.
   Minneapolis who?
Minneapolis each day
keep many doctors away.

Knock–knock.
   Who's there?
Mischief.
   Mischief who?
I guess I'd Mischief
(miss you if) you left . . .

Knock–knock.
   Who's there?
Miniature.
   Miniature who?
Miniature open your mouth,
you put your foot in it.

Knock–knock.
   Who's there?
Minnie.
   Minnie who?
No, not Minnie-who–
Minnehaha.

Knock–knock.
   Who's there?
Missouri.
   Missouri who?
Missouri (misery)
loves company!

Knock–knock.
Who's there?
Mohair.
Mohair who?
Any Mohair on your head and you could pass for a mop.

Knock–knock.
Who's there?
Morey and Les.
Morey and Les who?
The Morey I think of you, the Les I think of you.

Knock–knock.
Who's there?
Morgan.
Morgan who?
Morgan just a pretty face!

Knock–knock.
Who's there?
Mrs. S. Goode.
Mrs. S. Goode who?
A Mrs. S. Goode as a mile.

Knock–knock.
Who's there?
Mr. T.
Mr. T. who?
"Ah, sweet Mr. T. of life . . ."

Knock–knock.
   Who's there?
Murray Lee.
   Murray Lee who?
"Murray Lee we roll along . . ."

Knock–knock.
   Who's there?
Musket.
   Musket who?
Musket in! The Martians
are after me!

Knock–knock.
   Who's there?
Mussolini.
   Mussolini who?
Mussolini on your bell
for ten minutes.

Knock–knock.
   Who's there?
Mustard Bean.
   Mustard Bean who?
You Mustard Bean a big surprise
to your parents. They probably
expected a boy or girl.

Knock-Knock!

N

Knock–knock.
    Who's there?
Nanny.
    Nanny who?
Nanny my friends
like you either.

Knock–knock.
    Who's there?
Nanya.
    Nanya who?
Nanya Lip!

Knock–knock.
　　Who's there?
N.E.
　　N.E. who?
N.E. body you like, as
long as you let me in!

Knock–knock.
　　Who's there?
Needle.
　　Needle who?
Needle little attention.

　　Knock–knock.
　　　Who's there?
　Needle.
　　　Needle who?
　Needle little help!

Knock–knock.
>Who's there?

Nemo.
>Nemo who?

Nemo time to think
of a joke!

Knock–knock.
>Who's there?

Nefertiti.
>Nefertiti who?

Nefertiti (never teeter)
totter with a 500-pound
gorilla!

Knock–knock.
　Who's there?
Nevada.
　Nevada who?
You Nevada had it so good!

Knock–knock.
　Who's there?
Gouda.
　Gouda who?
This is as Goudas it gets!

Knock–knock.
　Who's there?
Osgood.
　Osgood who?
Osgood S. Canby.

Knock–knock.
　Who's there?
Nevil.
　Nevil who?
Nevil mind!

Knock–knock.
　Who's there?
Nevin.
　Nevin who?
Nevin you mind—
just open up.

Knock–knock.
　Who's there?
New Year.
　New Year who?
New Year (knew you were)
going to say that!

Knock–knock.
Who's there?
Noah.
Noah who?
There's Noah-scape!

Knock–knock.
Who's there?
Nobel.
Nobel who?
Nobel, so I knocked.

Knock–knock.
Who's there?
Noodle.
Noodle who?
Never Noodle now
where you lived.

Knock–knock.
Who's there?
Nora Marx.
Nora Marx who?
Nora Marx (no remarks) from
the peanut gallery!

Knock–knock.
Who's there?
Avery.
Avery who?
Avery body's gettin' into
the act!

Knock–knock.

Who's there?

Norma Lee.

Norma Lee who?

Norma Lee I don't go around knocking on doors, but I have this wonderful set of encyclopedias . . .

Knock–knock.

Who's there?

Nutmeg.

Nutmeg who?

Nutmeg any difference what you say.

Knock–knock.

Who's there?

Nuisance.

Nuisance who?

What's nuisance yesterday?

Knock–knock.

Who's there?

Nurse.

Nurse who?

Nurse sense in talking to you.

Knock-Knock!

Knock–knock.
Who's there?
Obi Wan.
Obi Wan who?
Obi Wan-derful and
take me to the movies!

Knock–knock.
Who's there?
O'Casey.
O'Casey who?
O'Casey if I care!

Knock–knock.
Who's there?
Odaris.
Odaris who?
Odaris a bee on your shoulder!

Knock–knock.
　Who's there?
Odd Thing.
　　Odd Thing who?
Odd Thing (I'd sing) all
day if I knew a thong!

Knock–knock.
　Who's there?
Odysseus.
(Pronounced Oh-diss-us).
　　Odysseus who?
Odysseus getting boring!

Knock–knock.
　Who's there?
Odysseus.
　　Odysseus who?
Odysseus the last straw!

Knock–knock.
　　Who's there?
Odyssey.
　　Odyssey who?
Odyssey (hard to see)
how you made it past
the first grade!

Knock–knock.
　Who's there?
Offer.
　　Offer who?
Offer got (I forgot)!

Knock–knock.
　Who's there?
Office.
　　Office who?
He's Office rocker.

166

Knock–knock.
  Who's there?
Ogre.
  Ogre who?
Ogre take a flying leap!

Knock–knock.
  Who's there?
Ohio.
  Ohio who?
Ohio feeling?

  Knock–knock.
    Who's there?
Kentucky.
    Kentucky who?
Kentucky (can't talk) too
well, have a soar throat.

  Knock–knock.
    Who's there?
Nevada.
    Nevada who?
Nevada saw you look worse.
You should be in bed.

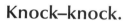

Knock–knock.
  Who's there?
Ohio.
  Ohio who?
Ohio Silver!

Knock–knock.
  Who's there?
Ohio.
  Ohio who?
Ohio feeling?

Knock–knock.
  Who's there?
Oink.
  Oink who?
Oink L. Sam!

Knock–knock.
Who's there?
O'Keefe.
O'Keefe who?
"O'Keefe me a home where the buffalo roam . . ."

Knock–knock.
Who's there?
Olga.
Olga who?
Olga home if you don't treat me better.

Knock–knock.
Who's there?
Olivia.
Olivia who?
Olivia (I live here) but I forgot my key.

Knock–knock.
Who's there?
Olivia.
Olivia who?
Olivia lone if that's
what you want!

Knock–knock.
Who's there?
Olivia.
Olivia who?
Olivia me alone!

Knock–knock.
Who's there?
Ollie-Lou.
Ollie-Lou who?
Ollie-Lou ya! You finally
opened the door!

Knock–knock.
Who's there?
Ollie or Rex.
Ollie or Rex who?
Don't put Ollie or Rex
in one basket.

Knock–knock.
   Who's there?
Omaha.
   Omaha who?
Omaha goodness! My hand
is caught in the door!

Knock–knock.
   Who's there?
Ollie.
   Ollie who?
Ollie time you say that,
I wish you'd cut it out.

Knock–knock.
   Who's there?
Omar.
   Omar who?
Omar goodness gracious!
Wrong door!

Knock–knock.
   Who's there?
Omega.
   Omega who?
Omega best man win!

Knock–knock.
   Who's there?
Omega.
   Omega who?
Omega up your mind.

Knock–knock.
Who's there?
Ooze.
Ooze who?
Ooze in charge
around here?

Knock–knock.
Who's there?
Opossum.
Opossum who?
Opossum by and
thought I'd say hello.

Knock–knock.
Who's there?
Orangutan.
Orangutan who?
Orangutan times but
you didn't answer.

Knock–knock.
Who's there?
Orbach.
Orbach who?
Front Orbach—
you look awful.

Knock–knock.
     Who's there?
Osaka.
     Osaka who?
Osaka to me!

Knock–knock.
     Who's there?
Oxford.
     Oxford who?
You Oxford it! (*Pow!*)

Knock–knock.
     Who's there?
Oscar and Greta.
     Oscar and Greta who?
Oscar foolish question and
Greta a foolish answer.

Knock–knock.
     Who's there?
O'Shea.
     O'Shea who?
O'Shea it isn't so.

Knock–knock.
     Who's there?
Oslo.
     Oslo who?
Oslo on cash.
How about a little loan?

Knock–knock.
   Who's there?
Otto B.
   Otto B. who?
Otto B. a law against people like you.

Knock–knock.
   Who's there?
Otto.
   Otto who?
Your bell is Otto order.

Knock–knock.
   Who's there?
Owen Williams.
   Owen Williams who?
Owen Williams
(oh, when will you)
open this door?

Knock–knock.
   Who's there?
Oz.
   Oz who?
Oz out here freezing.

Knock-Knock!

P

Knock–knock.
Who's there?
Panda.
Panda who?
Panda monium!

Knock–knock.
Who's there?
Passion.
Passion who?
Passion by and thought
I'd say hello.

Knock–knock.
Who's there?
Pasteur.
Pasteur who?
It's Pasteur (past your)
bedtime!

Knock–knock.
    Who's there?
Pasta.
    Pasta who?
Pasta pizza under the door—I'm starved!

Knock–knock.
    Who's there?
Azenauer.
    Azenauer who?
Azenauer (has an hour) gone by
since you put the pizza in the oven?

Knock–knock.
    Who's there?
Patton.
    Patton who?
Patton leather shoes!

Knock–knock.
    Who's there?
Paul.
    Paul who?
Paul-tergeist!

Knock–knock.
    Who's there?
Peapod.
    Peapod who?
I don't want to hear a
Peapod (peep out of) you!

Knock–knock.
Who's there?
Pekingese.
Pekingese who?
Pekingese through the peephole and see.

Knock–knock.
Who's there?
Phineas.
Phineas who?
Phineas thing happened on the way over here . . .

Knock–knock.
Who's there?
Percy.
Percy who?
Percy-veere (persevere)!

Knock–knock.
Who's there?
Phyllis.
Phyllis who?
Phyllis in on the details!

Knock–knock.
Who's there?
Pinafore.
Pinafore who?
Pinafore for your thoughts . . .

Knock–knock.
　　Who's there?
Pitcher.
　　Pitcher who?
Pitcher money where
your mouth is!

Knock–knock.
　　Who's there?
Pizza.
　　Pizza who?
Pizza nice guy when
you get to know him.

Knock–knock.
　　Who's there?
Plato.
　　Plato who?
Plato spaghetti and meatballs, please.

Knock–knock.
　　Who's there?
Police.
　　Police who?
Police open the door!

Knock–knock.
　　Who's there?
Police.
　　Police who?
Police B. Careful!

Knock–knock.
Who's there?
Polly N.
Polly N. who?
Polly N. saturated.

Knock–knock.
Who's there?
Possum.
Possum who?
Possum peace pipe.

Knock–knock.
Who's there?
Pumpkin.
Pumpkin who?
A thing that goes pumpkin (bump in) the night.

Knock–knock.
Who's there?
Porsche.
Porsche who?
Porsche me in the right direction!

Knock–knock.
Who's there?
Preston.
Preston who?
Preston the doorbell, but it won't ring.

Knock–knock.
Who's there?
Pudding.
Pudding who?
Pudding my best foot forward!

P

Knock–knock.
Who's there?
Punch.
Punch who?
Not me–
I just got here!

Knock–knock.
Who's there?
Pyrite.
Pyrite who?
Pyrite in your face—Pow!

Knock-Knock!

Knock–knock.
    Who's there?
Quacker.
    Quacker who?
Quacker 'nother bad joke
and I'm leaving.

Knock–knock.
    Who's there?
Quebec.
    Quebec who?
Quebec to the end
of the line.

Knock–knock.
    Who's there?
Quibble.
    Quibble who?
Quibble and Bits.

Knock–knock.
    Who's there?
Quiet Tina.
    Quiet Tina who?
Quiet Tina courtroom—
monkey wants to speak.

Knock–knock.
    Who's there?
Quigley.
    Quigley who?
Open the door Quigley,
I must get in!

Knock-Knock!

Knock–knock.
　　Who's there?
Radio.
　　Radio who?
Radio not, here
I come!

Knock–knock.
　　Who's there?
Raisin.
　　Raisin who?
Raisin Cane!

Knock–knock.
　　Who's there?
Rajah.
　　Rajah who?
Rajah Rabbit!

Knock–knock.
Who's there?
Ralph.
Ralph who?
Ralph! Ralph! I'm
a puppy dog!

Knock–knock.
Who's there?
Rambo.
Rambo who?
"Somewhere, over
the Rambo . . ."

Knock–knock.
Who's there?
Ramona.
Ramona who?
Ramona going to ask you
once more . . .

Knock–knock.
Who's there?
Randall.
Randall who?
Randall the way
from the bus.

Knock–knock.
Who's there?
Raoul (pronounced Rah-*ool*).
Raoul who?
"Raoul out the barrel . . ."

Knock–knock.
Who's there?
A Raven.
A Raven who?
A Raven Maniac.

Knock–knock.
Who's there?
Ray and Greta.
Ray and Greta who?
You'll Ray Greta asking
me that!

Knock–knock.
Who's there?
Rector.
Rector who?
Rector car. Can I
use your phone?

Knock–knock.
Who's there?
Renata.
Renata who?
Renata (run out of) steam?

Knock–knock.
Who's there?
Reverend.
Reverend who?
For Reverend ever I've
been standing out here . . .

Knock–knock.
Who's there?
Rhett.
Rhett who?
Rhett-urn of the Jedi.

Knock–knock.
Who's there?
Rhonda.
Rhonda who?
Rhonda arrest!

Knock–knock.
Who's there?
Rick.
Rick who?
Rick Shaw, hop in
for a ride!

Knock–knock.
Who's there?
Ringo.
Ringo who?
Ringo round the collar.

Knock–knock.
Who's there?
Ripon.
Ripon who?
Ripon up your welcome mat.

R

Knock–knock.
Who's there?
Rise and Follow.
Rise and Follow who?
Rise and Follow (rise and fall of) the Roman Empire.

Knock–knock.
Who's there?
Rita.
Rita who?
Rita my lips!

Knock–knock.
　Who's there?
Robert de Niro.
　Robert de Niro who?
Robert de Niro, but he's not here yet.

Knock–knock.
　Who's there?
Robert Redford.
　Robert Redford who?
Robert Redford the part in the play.

Knock–knock.
　Who's there?
Rollin.
　Rollin who?
"As we come rollin' rollin' home . . ."

Knock–knock.
　Who's there?
Roman.
　Roman who?
Roman around with nothing to do.

Knock–knock.
　Who's there?
Romanoff.
　Romanoff who?
There ain't Romanoff for the both of us in this town!

Knock–knock.
　Who's there?
Ronan.
　Ronan who?
Ronan amuck!

Knock–knock.
  Who's there?
Ron.
  Ron who?
Ron for your life!

Knock–knock.
  Who's there?
Rover.
  Rover who?
It's all Rover between us.

Knock–knock.
  Who's there?
Roxanne.
  Roxanne who?
Roxanne your head
or something?

Knock–knock.
  Who's there?
Rona.
  Rona who?
Rona the mill.

Knock–knock.
  Who's there?
Roy.
  Roy who?
Roy L. Flush!

Knock-knock.
　Who's there?
Rubber Duck.
　Rubber Duck who?
"Rubber Duck dub—
three men in a tub . . ."

Knock–knock.
　Who's there?
Rumania.
　Rumania who?
Can't Rumania out here
much longer.

Knock–knock.
　Who's there?
Rufus.
　Rufus who?
Rufus leaking and
I'm getting wet.

Knock–knock.
　Who's there?
Russ.
　Russ who?
Russ Crispies!

Knock-Knock!

S

Knock–knock.
Who's there?
Sadie.
Sadie who?
Sadie Pledge of
Allegiance.

Knock–knock.
Who's there?
Safari.
Safari who?
Safari so good.

Knock–knock.
Who's there?
Safaris.
Safaris who?
Safaris I can see,
it's me!

Knock–knock.
Who's there?
Salem.
Salem who?
Salem away for good–never have to see you again.

Knock–knock.
Who's there?
Sam and Janet.
Sam and Janet who?
"Sam and Janet evening, you will meet a stranger . . ."

Knock–knock.
Who's there?
Salada.
Salada who?
Salada bad Knock-Knock jokes around.

Knock–knock.
Who's there?
Sam.
Sam who?
Sam old story.
Ho-hum.

Knock–knock.
Who's there?
Samovar.
Samovar who?
Samovar time you can be a real pest.

Knock–knock.
Who's there?
Sancho.
Sancho who?
Sancho a letter, but
you never answered.

Knock–knock.
Who's there?
Sanctuary.
Sanctuary who?
Sanctuary much.

Knock–knock.
Who's there?
Santa Ana.
Santa Ana who?
Santa Ana coming
to your house because
you've been bad.

Knock–knock.
Who's there?
Santa.
Santa who?
Santa Mental Fool!

Knock–knock.
Who's there?
Santucci.
Santucci who?
Santucci my sunburn!

Knock–knock.
    Who's there?
Satin.
    Satin who?
Who Satin my chair?

Knock–knock.
Who's there?
Satellite.
Satellite who?
Satellite in the window—
one if by land,
two if by sea.

Knock–knock.
Who's there?
Sarah.
Sarah who?
Sarah doctor in
the house?

Knock–knock.
Who's there?
Sarong and Sari.
Sarong and Sari who?
Sarong house. Sari.

Knock–knock.
Who's there?
Sasha.
Sasha who?
Sasha dummy!

Knock–knock.
Who's there?
Saul and Terry.
Saul and Terry who?
Saul and Terry confinement!

Knock–knock.
Who's there?
Saul Upp.
Saul Upp who?
Saul Upp to you!

Knock–knock.
Who's there?
Schick.
Schick who?
I'm Schick as a dog.

Knock–knock.
Who's there?
Esau.
Esau who?
Esau throat is killing me.

Knock–knock.
Who's there?
Consuelo.
Consuelo who?
Consuelo a thing.

Knock–knock.
Who's there?
Gargoyle.
Gargoyle who?
Gargoyle with salt water
and you'll feel better.

Knock–knock.
Who's there?
Hatch.
Hatch who?
I didn't know you
were sick, too.

Knock–knock.
Who's there?
Schatzi.
Schatzi who?
Schatzi way the
ball bounces.

Knock–knock.
Who's there?
Schenectady.
Schenectady who?
Schenectady (the neck
of the) shirt is too tight.

Knock–knock.
Who's there?
Scissor.
Scissor who?
Scissor and Cleopatra.

Knock–knock.
Who's there?
Scoot.
Scoot who?
Scoot to be here!

Knock–knock.
Who's there?
Scold.
Scold who?
Scold outside.

Knock–knock.
Who's there?
Sea Bass.
Sea Bass who?
Sea Bass-tian the crab.

Knock–knock.
Who's there?
Scott.
Scott who?
Scott to be me!

Knock–knock.
   Who's there?
Seashell.
   Seashell who?
"Seashell have music
wherever she goes . . ."

Knock–knock.
   Who's there?
Seiko.
   Seiko who?
"Seiko and ye shall
find . . ."

Knock–knock.
   Who's there?
Seminole.
   Seminole who?
"Seminole cowhand–
from the Rio Grande . . ."

199

Knock–knock.
　　Who's there?
Senior.
　　Senior who?
Senior through the
peephole, so I know
you're in there.

Knock–knock.
　　Who's there?
Seth.
　　Seth who?
Seth me, that's who.

Knock–knock.
　　Who's there?
Seymour.
　　Seymour who?
Seymour if you'd get
the door open.

Knock–knock.
　　Who's there?
Shelley.
　　Shelley who?
Shelley try again?
　Knock–knock.
　　　Who's there?
Dozen.
　　Dozen who?
Dozen matter to me!

Knock–knock.
    Who's there?
Sheila.
    Sheila who?
"Sheila be coming
round the mountain
when she comes . . ."

Knock–knock.
    Who's there?
Sharon.
    Sharon who?
Sharon share alike.

Knock–knock.
    Who's there?
Shafter.
    Shafter who?
Shafter make a
phone call!

Knock–knock.
    Who's there?
Shirley M.
    Shirley M. who?
Shirley M. glad to say
goodbye to you.

Knock–knock.
Who's there?
Shoe buckle.
Shoe buckle who?
Shoe buckle up your seat belt?

Knock–knock.
Who's there?
Shoes.
Shoes who?
Shoes me, I must
have knocked on
the wrong door.

Knock–knock.
Who's there?
Shopper Dan.
Shopper Dan who?
You're Shopper Dan
(sharper than) I thought!

Knock–knock.
Who's there?
Siam.
Siam who?
Siam your old pal.

Knock–knock.
Who's there?
Sid.
Sid who?
"Sid-down, you're rocking the boat . . ."

Knock–knock.
Who's there?
Siamese.
Siamese who?
Siamese-y to please.

Knock–knock.

Who's there?

Sigrid.

Sigrid who?

Sigrid Service–
open up!

Knock–knock.

Who's there?

Simms.

Simms who?

Simms like I'm always
knocking on doors.

Knock–knock.

Who's there?

Simon.

Simon who?

"Simon the mood
for love . . ."

Knock–knock.

Who's there?

Sinatra.

Sinatra who?

Sinatra the cough
that carries you off,
it's the coffin they
carry you off in.

Knock–knock.

Who's there?

Sincerely.

Sincerely who?

Sincerely this morning
I've been listening to
Knock-Knock jokes.

Knock–knock.

Who's there?

Sis.

Sis who?

Sis any way to
treat a friend?

Knock–knock.
Who's there?
Sly Dover.
Sly Dover who?
Sly Dover, I'm breaking down the door!

Knock–knock.
Who's there?
Sodium.
Sodium who?
Sodium (so do you) mind if I come in?

Knock–knock.
Who's there?
Sloan.
Sloan who?
Sloan (slow and) steady wins the race!

Knock–knock.
Who's there?
Snow.
Snow who?
Snow use talking to you.

Knock–knock.
Who's there?
Sony.
Sony who?
Sony your old pal . . .
Knock–knock.
Who's there?
Trotter.
Trotter who?
Trotter remember me.

Knock–knock.
Who's there?
Sonny N.
Sonny N. who?
Sonny N. clear today–
rain tomorrow!

Knock–knock.
Who's there?
Sony and Toshiba.
Sony and Toshiba who?
Sony me, waiting Toshiba.

Knock–knock.
Who's there?
Spetzel.
Spetzel who?
Spetzel delivery!

Knock–knock.
Who's there?
Spook.
Spook who?
I spook too soon!

Knock–knock.
    Who's there?
Stan.
    Stan who?
Stan back–I'm knocking
the door down.

Knock–knock.
    Who's there?
Stan and Bea.
    Stan and Bea who?
Stan Dupp and Bea
Counted!

Knock–knock.
    Who's there?
Stella.
    Stella who?
Stella no answer
at the door.

Knock–knock.
    Who's there?
Stencil.
    Stencil who?
Stencil–there's a
bee on your nose.

Knock–knock.
    Who's there?
Sue.
    Sue who?
Sue-prise–it's me!

Knock–knock.
Who's there?
Sumatra.
Sumatra who?
What's Sumatra with you?

Knock–knock.
Who's there?
Sven.
Sven who?
Sven are you going
to open the door?

Knock–knock.
Who's there?
Swatter.
Swatter who?
Swatter you complaining
about now?

Knock–knock.
Who's there?
Surreal.
Surreal who?
Surreal pleasure
to be here!

Knock–knock.
Who's there?
Swann.
Swann who?
"Just Swann of those
things . . ."

Knock–knock.
Who's there?
Sybil.
Sybil who?
Sybil War!

Knock–knock.
Who's there?
Sycamore.
Sycamore who?
Sycamore Knock-Knock jokes.

Knock-Knock!

Knock–knock.
Who's there?
Tamara.
Tamara who?
Tamara Boom-dee-ay!

Knock–knock.
Who's there?
Tasmania.
Tasmania who?
Tasmania slip between
the cup and the lip.

Knock–knock.
Who's there?
Taurus.
Taurus who?
Taurus closed on
my foot. Ouch!

T

Knock–knock.
Who's there?
Tennessee.
Tennessee who?
Tennessee you tonight?

Knock–knock.
Who's there?
Tamara.
Tamara who?
Tamara would be better.

Knock–knock.
Who's there?
Tennessee.
Tennessee who?
Is that a Tennessee
(tan I see), or haven't
you bathed lately?

Knock–knock.
Who's there?
Terrify.
Terrify who?
Terrify tissue?

Knock–knock.
Who's there?
Tess Slater.
Tess Slater who?
Tess Slater than you think!

Knock–knock.

Who's there?

Thaddeus.

Thaddeus who?

Thaddeus the silliest thing I ever heard.

Knock–knock.

Who's there?

Thayer.

Thayer who?

Thayer thorry and I won't throw this pie in your face.

Knock–knock.

Who's there?

Thea.

Thea who?

Thea later, alligator.

Knock–knock.

Who's there?

Thelonius.

Thelonius who?

Thelonius kid in town.

Knock–knock.
Who's there?
The Genius.
The Genius who?
The Genius (the genie is)
out of the bottle.

Knock–knock.
Who's there?
The Ghost.
The Ghost who?
The Ghost is clear—
let's go!

Knock–knock.
Who's there?
Theodore.
Theodore who?
Theodore is closed,
open up!

Knock–knock.
Who's there?
Theonie.
Theonie who?
Theonie trouble with
your face is that it shows.

Knock–knock.
Who's there?
Theophilus.
Theophilus who?
Theophilus person I ever
met is you.

Knock–knock.
> Who's there?

Thistle.
> Thistle who?

Thistle be the last time
I knock on your door.

Knock–knock.
> Who's there?

Theresa.
> Theresa who?

Theresa fly in my soup.

Knock–knock.
> Who's there?

Threadbare.
> Threadbare who?

Threadbare-n (the Red Baron)
and Snoopy the Flying Ace.

Knock–knock.
> Who's there?

Thud.
> Thud who?

Thud you'd never ask!

Knock–knock.
> Who's there?

Thurston.
> Thurston who?

Thurston for some water.

Knock–knock.
Who's there?
Tibet.
Tibet who?
Early Tibet and
early to rise . . .

Knock–knock.
Who's there?
Tick.
Tick who?
Tick 'em up!

Knock–knock.
Who's there?
Tijuana.
Tijuana who?
Tijuana try for two
out of three?

Knock–knock.
Who's there?
Tinker Bell.
Tinker Bell who?
Tinker Bell is out of
order.

Knock–knock.
Who's there?
Titus.
Titus who?
Titus string around your
finger so you won't forget
to open the door.

Knock–knock.
Who's there?
Toby.
Toby who?
Toby or not Toby.

Knock–knock.
Who's there?
Thaddeus.
Thaddeus who?
Thaddeus question.

T

Knock–knock.
Who's there?
Toad.
Toad who?
Toad you before,
but you forgot.

Knock–knock.
Who's there?
Tobias.
Tobias who?
Are you going Tobias more
Knock-Knock books.

Knock–knock.
Who's there?
Toledo.
Toledo who?
It's easy Toledo horse to water,
but you can't make him drink.

Knock–knock.
　Who's there?
Tom Hills.
　Tom Hills who?
Tom Hills (time heals)
all wounds!

Knock–knock.
　Who's there?
Tommy.
　Tommy who?
I have a Tommy Ache!

Knock–knock.
　Who's there?
Toodle-oo.
　Toodle-oo who?
"Skip Toodle-oo,
my darling . . ."

Knock–knock.
　Who's there?
Toodle.
　Toodle who?
Bye-bye.

Knock–knock.
Who's there?
Toothache.
　Toothache who?
Toothache the high road
and I'll take the low road.

Knock–knock.
　Who's there?
Top Hat.
　Top Hat who?
Top Hat (stop that–
you're bothering me!

Knock–knock.
　Who's there?
Topeka.
　Topeka who?
Don't open the door.
I like Topeka through
keyholes.

Knock–knock.
　Who's there?
Topol.
　Topol who?
"On Topol Old
Smokey . . ."

Knock–knock.
 Who's there?
Toreador.
 Toreador who?
Toreador down–now can I come in?

Knock–knock.
 Who's there?
Toronto.
 Toronto who?
Have Toronto the store.
Can I get you anything?
 Knock–knock.
 Who's there?
Canada.
 Canada who?
Canada best dog food.

Knock–knock.
 Who's there?
Toulouse.
 Toulouse who?
Want Toulouse ten ugly
pounds? Cut off your head.

Knock–knock.
   Who's there?
Trigger.
   Trigger who?
Trigger treat!

Knock–knock.
   Who's there?
Troy.
   Troy who?
Troy as I may,
I can't reach the bell.

Knock–knock.
   Who's there?
Troy.
   Troy who?
Troy again!
   Knock–knock.
      Who's there?
   Wes D.
      Wes D. who?
   Wes D. point?

Knock–knock.
   Who's there?
Trudy.
   Trudy who?
Can I come Trudy window?
The door is stuck.

Knock–knock.
    Who's there?
Truman E.
    Truman E. who?
Truman E. cooks spoil
the broth!

Knock–knock.
    Who's there?
Turner.
    Turner who?
Turner round. You look
better from the back.

Knock–knock.
    Who's there?
Two badgers.
    Two badgers who?
Two badgers got a chip
on your shoulder.

Knock-Knock!

U

Knock–knock.
 Who's there?
U-Boat.
 U-Boat who?
U-Boat me a present?

Knock–knock.
 Who's there?
Udall.
 Udall who?
Udall know if you
opened the door.

Knock–knock.
Who's there?
Udder.
Udder who?
Udder Lee ridiculous!

Knock–knock.
Who's there?
Uganda.
Uganda who?
Uganda be kidding me!

Knock–knock.
Who's there?
Uganda.
Uganda who?
Uganda get away
with this.

Knock–knock.
Who's there?
Uganda.
Uganda who?
Uganda never guess.

Knock–knock.
Who's there?
Unaware.
Unaware who?
Your unaware has a hole in it!

Knock–knock.
Who's there?
Tom Sawyer.
Tom Sawyer who?
Tom Sawyer underwear.

Knock–knock.
Who's there?
Arkansas.
Arkansas who?
Arkansas it, too!

Knock–knock.
Who's there?
Esau.
Esau who?
Esau it too.

Knock–knock.
  Who's there?
Unique.
  Unique who?
Why do Unique
(you sneak)
around on tiptoe?

Knock–knock.
  Who's there?
Unicorn.
  Unicorn who?
Unicorn-iest guy I ever met.

U

Knock–knock.
  Who's there?
Unity.
  Unity who?
Unity sweater for me?

Knock–knock.
  Who's there?
Upton.
  Upton who?
Upton no good,
as usual.

Knock–knock.
  Who's there?
Ural.
  Ural who?
Ural washed up, kid!

Knock–knock.
  Who's there?
Uriah.
  Uriah who?
Keep Uriah on the ball.

Knock–knock.
  Who's there?
Uruguay.
  Uruguay who?
You go Uruguay and
I'll go mine.

Knock–knock.
  Who's there?
Usher.
  Usher who?
Usher wish you would
let me in.

Knock–knock.
  Who's there?
Utah-Nevada.
  Utah-Nevada who?
Utah-Nevada guessed if
I didn't tell you.

Knock–knock.
     Who's there?
Uta.
     Uta who?
Uta sight, uta mind.

Knock–knock.
     Who's there?
Uta May.
     Uta May who?
Going Uta May mind!

Knock–knock.
     Who's there?
Utica.
     Utica who?
Utica high road and I'll
take the low road.

Knock-Knock!

V

Knock–knock.
Who's there?
Vacancy.
Vacancy who?
Vacancy (we can see)
right in your window!

Knock–knock.
Who's there?
Valley.
Valley who?
Valley intellesting!

Knock–knock.
Who's there?
Vanna White.
Vanna White who?
Vanna White (want to
write) your name on this
dotted line?

Knock–knock.
Who's there?
Vasilli.
Vasilli who?
Vasilli (what a silly)
person you are!

Knock–knock.
Who's there?
Van Gogh.
Van Gogh who?
Ready–set–Van Gogh!

Knock–knock.
Who's there?
Vaudeville.
Vaudeville who?
Vaudeville (what will)
you be doing tonight?

Knock–knock.
Who's there?
Vaughan.
Vaughan who?
Vaughan to come
over tomorrow?

Knock–knock.
Who's there?
Vassar girl.
Vassar girl who?
Vassar girl like you doing
in a place like this?

Knock–knock.
Who's there?
Vaughan.
Vaughan who?
"Vaughan day my
prince will come . . ."

Knock–knock.
Who's there?
Veal chop.
Veal chop who?
Veal chop for a used car.

Knock–knock.
Who's there?
Vehicle.
Vehicle who?
Don't call us–
Vehicle (we will call) you!

Knock–knock.
Who's there?
Ventriloquist.
Ventriloquist who?
Ventriloquist-mas tree
get decorated?

Knock–knock
Who's there?
Venice.
Venice who?
Venice these Knock-Knock
jokes going to stop?

Knock–knock.
Who's there?
Venus.
Venus who?
Venus see you,
I feel sick.

Knock–knock.
Who's there?
Veronica.
Veronica who?
Veronica (we're on a c-)razy diet.

Knock–knock.
    Who's there?
Vera.
    Vera who?
"Vera all the flowers
gone . . ."

Knock–knock.
    Who's there?
Vi.
    Vi who?
Vi not?!

Knock–knock.
    Who's there?
Vicious.
    Vicious who?
Best Vicious!

Knock–knock.
    Who's there?
Vienna.
    Vienna who?
Zis is Vienna the book.

Knock–knock.
    Who's there?
Vile.
    Vile who?
Vile the cat's away,
the mice vill play!

Knock–knock.
    Who's there?
Vilma.
    Vilma who?
Vilma frog turn
into a prince?

Knock–knock.
    Who's there?
Vilma.
    Vilma who?
Vilma dreams come true?

Knock–knock.
   Who's there?
Viola.
   Viola who?
Viola sudden you
don't know me?

Knock–knock.
   Who's there?
Violet.
   Violet who?
Violet the cat out
of the bag?

Knock–knock.
   Who's there?
Virtue.
   Virtue who?
Virtue get those big,
brown eyes?

Knock–knock.
   Who's there?
Virus.
   Virus who?
Virus you always
singing stupid songs?

Knock–knock.
   Who's there?
Viscount.
(Pronounced V-eye-count)
   Viscount who?
Viscount you behave?

Knock–knock.
   Who's there?
Voodoo.
   Voodoo who?
Voodoo you think you
are, the Wolf Man?

Knock-Knock!

W

Knock–knock.
Who's there?
Waco (pronounced Wake-o)
and El Paso.
Waco and El Paso who?
If I can stay Waco for the test,
I think El Paso.

Knock–knock.
Who's there?
Wallaby.
Wallaby who?
Wallaby in trouble
if I keep knocking
on the door?

Knock–knock.
Who's there?
Walter D.
Walter D. who?
Walter D. Lawn.

Knock–knock.
Who's there?
Waddle.
Waddle who?
Waddle I need to
do to get you to use
your brain?

Knock–knock.
Who's there?
Waiter.
Waiter who?
Waiter-ound and
you'll see!

Knock–knock.
Who's there?
Wadsworth.
Wadsworth who?
Wadsworth it to you if
I go away?

Knock–knock.
Who's there?
Wanamaker.
Wanamaker who?
Wanamaker mud pie?

Knock–knock.
Who's there?
Wanda.
Wanda who?
Wanda come out
and play?

Knock–knock.
Who's there?
Wanda.
Wanda who?
Wanda these days—Pow!

W

Knock–knock.
Who's there?
Warden.
Warden who?
Warden the world
are you up to?

Knock–knock.
Who's there?
Warner.
Warner who?
Warner you coming
out to play?

Knock–knock.
Who's there?
Warren.
Warren who?
Warren my birthday suit.

Knock–knock.
Who's there?
Warren.
Warren who?
I'm Warren out!

Knock–knock.
Who's there?
Warren D.
Warren D. who?
Warren D. world are you?

Knock–knock.
Who's there?
Warrior.
Warrior who?
Warrior been all my life?

Knock–knock.
  Who's there?
Warsaw.
  Warsaw who?
Warsaw Knock-Knock
joke I ever heard.

W

Knock–knock.
  Who's there?
Wash out.
  Wash Out who?
Wash Out, I'm coming in!

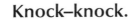

Knock–knock.
  Who's there?
Wash.
  Wash who?
Wash you there,
Charlie?

Knock–knock.
  Who's there?
Water.
  Water who?
Water be ashamed of yourself
for living in a dump like this!

Knock–knock.
Who's there?
Water.
Water who?
Water friends for?

Knock–knock.
Who's there?
Watts.
Watts who?
Watts up, Doc?

Knock–knock.
Who's there?
Wayne.
Wayne who?
I'm Wayne D. Outfield.

Knock–knock.
Who's there?
Weasel.
Weasel who?
"Weasel while you work . . ."

W

Knock–knock.
Who's there?
Wednesday.
Wednesday who?
"Wednesday saints go marching in . . ."

Knock–knock.
Who's there?
Weirdo.
Weirdo who?
Weirdo you think you're going?

Knock–knock.
Who's there?
Welcome.
Welcome who?
Welcome up and see me sometime.

Knock–knock.
Who's there?
Wendy.
Wendy who?
"Wendy wind blows, the cradle will rock . . ."

Knock–knock.
Who's there?
Wendy Katz.
Wendy Katz who?
Wendy Katz away, the
mice will play.

Knock–knock.
Who's there?
Wheelbarrow.
Wheelbarrow who?
Wheelbarrow some
money and go on a trip.

Knock–knock.
Who's there?
Whitmore.
Whitmore who?
Whitmore can I say
after I say I'm sorry?

Knock–knock.
Who's there?
Whitney.
Whitney who?
Whitney have to say
to me?

Knock–knock.
Who's there?
Werner.
Werner who?
Werner you going
to grow up?

Knock–knock.
Who's there?
Whelan.
Whelan who?
That's all Whelan
good, but I still think
you're a nut.

Knock–knock.
Who's there?
Whittier.
Whittier who?
Whittier think my
chances are for
getting inside?

Knock–knock.
　Who's there?
Who.
　Who who?
Terrible echo in here,
isn't there?

Knock–knock.
　Who's there?
Widow.
　Widow who?
A widow kid.

Knock–knock.
　Who's there?
Willard.
　Willard who?
Willard be too late if I
come back in an hour?

Knock–knock.
　Who's there?
Wiener.
　Wiener who?
Wiener takes all.

Knock–knock.
Who's there?
William Tell.
　William Tell who?
William Tell your mommy
to come to the door?

Knock–knock.
Who's there?
Will F.
Will F. who?
Will F. Iron.

Knock–knock.
Who's there?
Willoughby.
Willoughby who?
Willoughby my
Valentine?

Knock–knock.
Who's there?
Willie.
Willie who?
Willie or won't he?

Knock–knock.
Who's there?
Wilson.
Wilson who?
Wilson body let me in?

Knock–knock.
Who's there?
Winnie.
Winnie who?
Winnie you going to
open the door?

Knock–knock.
Who's there?
Winott.
Winott who?
Winott leave your
brain to science?
Maybe they can
find a cure for it.

Knock-knock.

Who's there?

Wire.

Wire who?

Wire we telling Knock-Knock jokes?

Knock–knock.

Who's there?

Wooden.

Wooden who?

Wooden you like to know!

Knock–knock.

Who's there?

Wienie.

Wienie who?

Wienie more jokes like these!

Knock–knock.

Who's there?

Archibald.

Archibald who?

Archibald real tears when he read these Knock-Knock jokes.

W

Knock–knock.
　　Who's there?
Wolf.
　　Wolf who?
Wolf-er goodness sake,
Grandma, what
big teeth you
have!

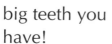

Knock–knock.
　　Who's there?
Woody.
　　Woody who?
Woody lady of the house
please open the door?

Knock–knock.
　　Who's there?
Woody.
　　Woody who?
Woody you care
who this is?

Knock–knock.
Who's there?
Wyatt.
Wyatt who?
Wyatt the world do I
bother to talk to you?

Knock–knock.
Who's there?
Wyden.
Wyden who?
Wyden you tell me
you were a werewolf?

Knock–knock.
Who's there?
Wynn.
Wynn who?
Wynn a few–lose a few.

Knock-Knock!

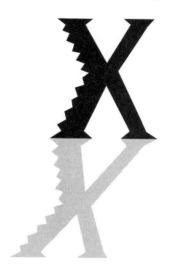

Knock–knock.
> Who's there?

X.
> X who?

X (Eggs) Benedict!

Knock–knock.
> Who's there?

X.
> X who?

X (Eggs) for breakfast.

Knock–knock.
> Who's there?

Xavier.
> Xavier who?

Xavier breath!
I'm not leaving.

Knock–knock.
> Who's there?

Xavier.
> Xavier who?

Xavier self!

Knock–knock.
Who's there?
Xenia.
Xenia who?
Xenia open the door
last week!

Knock–knock.
Who's there?
Oh Mama!
Oh Mama who?
Oh Mama-stake
(oh, my mistake)!

Knock–knock.
Who's there?
Xenia.
Xenia who?
Xenia stealing my
Mad Magazine.

Knock-Knock!

Y

Knock–knock.
　Who's there?
Yates.
　　Yates who?
Crazy Yates (Eights)!

Knock–knock.
　　Who's there?
Yeti.
　　Yeti who?
Yeti-nother Knock-Knock joke!

Knock–knock.
　Who's there?
Yogurt.
　　Yogurt who?
Yogurt to be joking!

Knock–knock.
　　Who's there?
Arno.
　　Arno who?
Arno you don't!

Knock–knock.
Who's there?
Yoko.
Yoko who?
Yoko jump in the lake.

Knock–knock.
Who's there?
Yokohama.
Yokohama who?
Yokohama (you can have my) place in line!

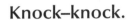

Knock–knock.
Who's there?
Yucatan.
Yucatan who?
Yucatan dollars to pay the taxi?

Knock–knock.
Who's there?
Yokum.
Yokum who?
"Yokum a long way, baby . . ."

Knock–knock.
Who's there?
Yucca.
Yucca who?
Yucca be arrested for impersonating a human being.

Knock–knock.
Who's there?
Yukon.
Yukon who?
Yukon (you can't) teach an old dog new tricks!

Y

Knock–knock.
    Who's there?
Yolette.
    Yolette who?
Would Yolette me in the door, please?

    Knock–knock.
        Who's there?
Wilma.
    Wilma who?
Wilma jokes make you open the door?

        Knock–knock.
        Who's there?
Ozzie.
    Ozzie who?
Ozzie (I see) I'm going to be out
here all night.

            Knock–knock.
            Who's there?
Yukon.
        Yukon who?
Yukon say that again!

Knock–knock.
  Who's there?
Yul.
  Yul who?
Yul look wonderful.
Who is your embalmer?

Knock–knock.
  Who's there?
Yule.
  Yule who?
Yule never guess.

Knock–knock.
  Who's there?
Yuma.
  Yuma who?
The Good Yuma man.

Knock–knock.
  Who's there?
Yuri.
  Yuri who?
Yuri mind me of
the Liberty Bell–
half-cracked.

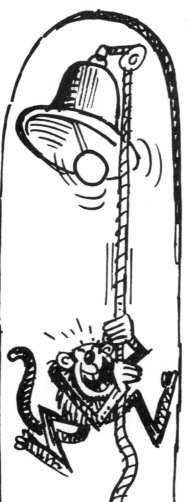

Knock-Knock!

Knock–knock.
    Who's there?
Zany.
    Zany who?
Zany body out there?!

Knock–knock.
    Who's there?
Zelda.
    Zelda who?
Zelda family jewels!

Knock–knock.
    Who's there?
Zenka.
    Zenka who?
Zenka you for your
kind words.

Knock–knock.
Who's there?
Zinc.
Zinc who?
Zinc or swim!

Knock–knock.
Who's there?
Zinc.
Zinc who?
Zinc of you all
the time!

Knock–knock.
Who's there?
Zinnia.
Zinnia who?
There's method
Zinnia madness.

Knock–knock.
Who's there?
Zipper and Zipper.
Zipper and Zipper who?
"Zipper D. Doodah and Zipper D.A. . . ."

Z

Knock–knock.
    Who's there?
Zits.
    Zits who?
Zits down and
concentrate.

Knock–knock.
    Who's there?
Zoe.
    Zoe who?
Zoe (so we)
meet again!

Knock–knock.
    Who's there?
Zoo.
    Zoo who?
Zoo long for now!
    Knock–knock.
        Who's there?
Cy.
    Cy who?
Cy O'Nara
(Sayonara)!

Knock–knock.
    Who's there?
Zuccarelli.
    Zuccarelli who?
Zuccarelli long time
to get to the last
Knock-Knock
joke!

INDEX